I0157180

*The **Sand Grit** in the Oyster **that Makes the Pearl***

On **Marriage & Buddhism**

(Being 60)

Patricia Mellencamp

Book III of **Aging and Amateur Knowledge**

Pell-Mell Publishing, 2017

To Jonathan Pellegrin,
my leading man and sparring partner
&
Dae and Rob Mellencamp,
my supporting players

with all my love and gratitude

Melodrama in Morocco

In March 2001, I was in Morocco -- in Marrakesh, an exotic, dramatic setting -- with Jonathan, whom I had known for only six, albeit intense, weeks. Despite the curious glances of the other diners, I was sobbing, pathetically. He looked stunned, bewildered. We were having lunch beside the pool of the magnificent Hotel Mamounia, where we were staying. So why was I crying? In such a perfect setting? The answer is embarrassing, but here it is, in context.

We had toured this wondrous country for twelve days, exploring the ancient Medinas of Fez, Rabat, Meknes, and Marrakesh -- and driving by ourselves through the countryside of tranquil farmland. The Medinas are the old central cities, dense warrens of artisans and their beautiful wares, trade, and the energy of crowded communal life.

Fez, the oldest city, dating back to 808, is a medieval Islamic city, extraordinarily beautiful. Dotted with gigantic palms and green domes, Fez is surrounded by mountains and streams running down to the fairytale city. The white houses with flat roofs have fine minarets made out of mosaic tiles. But even with a map, we became instantly lost in the intricate maze of the old city within five minutes, so we hired a guide, who wore an outer robe with a hood.

It was hard not to notice that women were largely missing in public places – the coffee houses and outdoor cafes were filled with men talking, hanging out, importantly so. When women did appear, they wore long, hooded gowns of many designs, jalabis, over their clothes. In the villages and countryside, women also wore veils over their faces. Houses were designed to

1

surround interior courtyards, where women worked, kept out of sight. I had never been in an Islamic culture.

After a few days, I began to feel uncomfortable in public spaces. And I was wearing my long skirts and long sleeve/high neck tops. I understood the protective anonymity of the jalabi (djellaba, jalaba), a garb also worn by many men. By not wearing it, I also felt as if I were flaunting the country's customs – Muslim traditions – and I did not want to be disrespectful to another culture or spiritual system.

I had been inspired by the philosophy of the Sufi poets and mystics, Rumi and Hafez.[1] Gurumayi Chidvilasananda, my spiritual teacher, often quoted the Islamic poet saints, Kabir and Rabbia[2]; or told the comic tales of Nasrudin. I had read several books of poetry, biographies, and scholarly analyses of Rumi's poetry and life.[3] One day I would make a pilgrimage to Rumi's shrine, in Konya, Turkey and attend a ceremony of the whirling dervishes, the Sufi dance of entrancement and adoration of God.

I recalled these books and the Sufi version of love as I traveled through Morocco. My amateur, beginner's knowledge of Islam made the strange less so. My knowledge was comforting to me, linking me just a little bit to the culture. I always responded to the call to prayer and took time to bow to Mecca. I found the haunting public prayers a beautiful reminder of our divinity, of a passionate faith in God, and of a historical lineage that had passed on these beliefs and practices through the generations.[4] The past became the present.

Time slipped into reverse. It could have been 1940 in the country, or even centuries ago in the Medinas of Fez, or Marrakesh. Most of the products were hand crafted; the wood and stone carving and inlays were intricate, carried over on a grand scale to the fretted architecture of minarets. In the countryside, farmers tilled the fields with a wooden plow and donkey. Stone fences decorated the landscape. We were in a country of natural and architectural beauty. It was the setting for a fairy tale, yet one that was real and very tangible.

But with each new five star hotel suite, in Fez or Rabat, one more luxurious than the previous, I became more anxious. At each checkpoint, I had insisted on showing my passport to the hotel clerk, rather than letting Jonathan handle it, which was logical because he had taken care of the reservations. He began to become irritated with what was becoming obvious – I didn't want him to see my passport. Why? His suspicion, so far in check, began to verge on anger.

To explain his frustration, he told me a poignant and troubling story of discovering a dreadful family scandal in the microfilm archives of the local newspaper when he was eighteen. Although he had repeatedly asked about how his grandfather had died, his mother had never told him the gruesome story: that (when she was 17) her father had shot and killed his business partner (who had been cheating him) and then himself. However, she had shared this tale of murder and suicide with his older brother, Dave. As a result, when information was withheld from Jonathan, he felt excluded, unworthy of confidentiality. This pain triggered anger, which he was trying to contain, barely.

What horrible fact was I trying to hide from him? Who was I? Was my passport a forgery? The jig was up. I confessed. "I'm 60," I sobbed. "What?" He looked bewildered. I repeated, "I'm 60." "Is that it? Why is that a problem? What's wrong with that?" He gently laughed, and his incredulity was genuine, he didn't care in the least that I was sixty, but I did. – I didn't like "being sixty," not at all. To compound my embarrassment, I had

3

fudged the dates of my high school and college graduations during our many long conversations, taking me down to a presumed and more acceptable 58, closer to his 56 years.

My recent birthday had not been a happy one for me. In fact, I was upset that I was sixty. It felt as if the best part of my life had already happened and the rest was downhill or on hold, a future to be lived in a dull, drab neutral. Who cared about 60 year old women? No one, I decided, not even other 60-year-old women.

Now 70, that would be another story – the story of *afterward* . . . after children, career ambition, physical attractiveness, and men (although I had already given them up there was still potential if not reality). 70 would be a landmark of letting go, followed by the glorious and eccentric 80s and the wizening of the 90s, into the frail ethereality of the 100s. 60, on the other hand, was just the dull beginning of the end.

Another trigger was something Jonathan said at our initial meeting at Columbia Hospital, just weeks earlier. After reading me a letter detailing his goals for the remainder of his life – no small surprise when he pulled out this intimate, typed document, along with an Excel spreadsheet of all his business commitments for the year! -- he invited me to visit him in Florida, soon. He didn't want to waste any time. It was urgent that he get on with his life because in four years he would be sixty! He repeated SIXTY!! as if it were a death knell, the resolute end. And I had just turned his dreaded sixty! Nine days earlier.

But I didn't tell him this. In fact, I dodged every age-related question, smudging and fudging and hemming and hawing even my graduation year from high school. I didn't lie, exactly, but I also didn't fess up.

My intense, morbid reaction to being sixty surprised me. I had written about the double standard of age wherein older men, in life and at the movies, retain their power and sexuality while older women lose theirs. Women could be fifty, but they had to look thirty. I hadn't considered sixty. And then there was the familiar scenario in life and in film of the older man and the younger woman as the central couple or story, rarely the inverse.

At the movies, in the boardroom, and in the halls of Congress, older men were still leading men whereas older women simply vanished. Where were they?[5]

Through my spiritual practices, I had disengaged the equation of self with body, or so I thought. Women are so much more than their bodies! Just sacks of skin which become slack with age. *I am not my skin!* And why are lines on women's faces and marks on their bodies any less attractive than those on men's skin? Why does Robert Redford get to have scars on his face? And still be attractive? Influential? Why does Jack Nicholson get to be fat, bald, and out of shape? And still be desirable? And powerful? (Years later, Jonathan let me know that he had noticed every sign of an aging body but accepted them as "part of the package.")

Although I was surprised by the negative emotions raised by the number, 60, I do think there is a landmark quality to 60 – with it comes the realization that life is about two-thirds or more over. Now we have old age and death ahead, and most of us are ill prepared for this awareness.

My distress was also magnified or triggered by being dumped on my 60th birthday by mustached Bob, the first man I had dated in many years.

A brief history . . . After my divorce in 1975, I loved the freedom of being single, although being a divorced parent to two children had its trials and terrors. I had a series of intense, short-term encounters, in the end, sabotaging every one. I could not sustain desire, after the initial romance. It took too much energy – and mine was used up by my life. Solution? Have quick, uncommitted relationships and at the first sign of dullness, flagging interest, conflict, or criticism, *particularly criticism*, break them off. Or better yet, slyly fix up your dates with your friends. The perfection of this defense was to eliminate intimate relationships altogether via a pre-emptive strike, while maintaining friendships.

One part of my ego was protected, invincible. The other part was too dependent on my children for affection. Later I would learn about my arrested emotions, their destructive nature.

After my children left for college in 1988, I learned to enjoy being and living alone. I began a period of life-changing discovery of what I call my amateur knowledges – of the twelve steps of AA and the principles of Eastern meditation – and achievement, publishing four scholarly books between 1990 and 1996 and becoming a Distinguished Professor. For seven years as I cared for my ailing parents, who moved a block from me in 1990, I dedicated myself to teaching, writing, AA meetings, and to my meditation practice. Being alone and enjoying the small pleasures, a book in bed, coffee in the quiet early morning, became precious to me. They still are.

So, there I am, in 1999, twenty five years single, the last fourteen of them dateless, teaching, writing, and living alone, a story of happily ever after very different from the coupled ending of so many Hollywood movies I had so archly analyzed in my recent book, **A Fine Romance: Five Ages of Film Feminism**.

My children had become delightful adults with graduate degrees, and professional careers. Dae had just been married in New York, in a moving Jewish wedding, and was enjoying her career in internet businesses – after receiving her MBA from Columbia. Rob was working as a computer engineer in Silicon Valley and studying for his third graduate degree, this time at UC/Berkeley. I had just negotiated a one-semester teaching load, along with a year's sabbatical and a big raise. Finally my salary was commensurate with my lofty title, Distinguished Professor.

I began to look for (and would soon buy) a second home on the coast of California, north of San Francisco where Rob lived. I was also looking for a condo in Manhattan. My future would be bi-coastal, an exciting conclusion to an entire life lived in the Midwest, in Wisconsin.

For the first time in my life, I could financially relax. My parents had left me a healthy stock portfolio. I could be writing and teaching at the University for the next 25 years – a bit of a daunting prospect yet nevertheless the easy, uneventful, and unemotional ending I foresaw for my life. The play had been cast and the major players had already made their appearances. There would be no big surprises, just some changes in the supporting roles. My life wasn't perfect, but it was fine to terrific. And I felt a bit superior to women who still "needed" or defined their happiness by men. (To be honest, it was more than "a bit.")

In fact, I had become Jessica Fletcher in the old TV series, **Murder She Wrote.** While her friends had dreadful marital feuds, often resulting in gruesome murders she would single-handedly solve, she was independent, above the emotional, destructive fray of marriage and the family. The TV series' star was, of course, an older woman, Angela Lansbury playing this mystery writer/sleuth.[6] Although she had admirers, she was never interested. A strong woman indeed!

But then in 1999 Italian Bob invited me to a movie. After fourteen dateless years, I accepted, with trepidation. It was a nervous evening, and I was home by 9 p.m. Whew! But I was attracted to him. He was a leader of our meditation center, where I had met him, ten years earlier. And a cook, with a pizza restaurant outside Milwaukee. He would help me on my spiritual path! And cook! What more could anyone need?

In his mid-fifties, short, attractive, in good shape, and never married, Bob had a reputation as a ladies man, but after each fling ended, he would return to Deanna, who had been rudely dumped and then reclaimed nine times. "Not me," said the Great Me, believing I was a cut above the previous dumpees. My logic, along with my outsized ego, was deeply flawed.

A little more than a year of anxiety and dissatisfaction later, after he returned from two weeks at **my** house in Sea Ranch, California, which I had purchased in December, 1999, Bob called me. It was January 15th, 2001, my 60th birthday. Rather than "Happy Birthday" and dinner plans, he told me about the Sufi massage therapist he had met in Sea Ranch, through our friends there. "I love her, she is The One."[7]

I was furious. *"The One?"* Something clicked, like a lamp in a dark room. Finally! In a burst of physical strength, I hauled his few possessions out of my condominium, to the garage. I needed to erase any sign of him from my life. It was sub-zero and snowy in Milwaukee in mid-January. Three hours later, I called Bob back, and quietly informed him that anything he didn't pick up **today**, the Salvation Army would, tomorrow. He asked for an extra day. I refused. And that was the end of Bob. No discussion. No shouting. No hysteria.

But there was emotional residue. How could I have been so egotistical to believe that I was better than other women? How did I so misunderstand what being "spiritual" means? It is an inner state, not outward ritual.

He also left his little and feisty black dog, 7 month old Rishi, not willing to care for her – but this turned out to be my great gift. She went everywhere with me.

I wanted to get over this quickly so I did something I had never done – I relinquished my pride. I brazenly told everyone I spoke to that Bob had dumped me. If I didn't run into someone, I called with the dump news. I didn't die of embarrassment or humiliation or not being good enough. Quite the contrary, I began to feel relief and a bit of humor. In the overall scheme of my life, this was not even a flyspeck. Not surprisingly, no one was unhappy with my news, particularly Rob and Dae, who tried not to shout with glee.

Increased meditation and chanting helped immeasurably. Charlotte Jocko Beck's book, **Nothing Special**, took care of the any aftereffects. I read sections of it every morning, after meditation. This little book set the emotional stage for what was to come next. For rather than burying or running away from pain, I learned to acknowledge and lean into it – as I had done with Rob's medical issue and my parents' deaths. But this time I did it with something ordinary and worldly.

The invincible part of my ego that had protected me from criticism and rejection would be exposed and very vulnerable. I was out there in the world, my defenses down in an almost breathless honesty. Paradoxically, I would soon learn, this made me infinitely stronger.

Charlotte Joko Beck taught at the San Diego Zen Center – but I have met her only in her two books. Her history is exceptional *and* typical. As the author of the preface tells us, she was born in New Jersey, went to college, married and had children. After her divorce, she "supported herself and her four children as a teacher, secretary, and later as an administrative assistant in a large university department." That was when Beck began to study Zen with a teacher in Los Angeles, commuting for years. She was designated his Dharma Heir, and in 1983 began to teach Zen in San Diego. "She no longer shaves her head, and seldom uses robes or her titles." (vi) She sees herself "as a guide rather than a guru, refusing to be put on a pedestal of any kind . . . she shares her own life difficulties." (vii) Which is why this is the first Zen book I have truly grasped.

In "Love," Beck takes a concept from a Zen scholar, Menzan Zenji (1683-1796) – *emotion-thought*, which she describes as *"self-centered thoughts that we fuss with all the time."* (71) I was familiar with fussing with 'self-centered thoughts,' along with my research and writing on anxiety. *"Their absence is the enlightened state,"* what Zen calls *satori*. I have had glimpses of this serene tranquility and clarity. But it never lasted. Beck goes on to define what she calls "false love," which resembles romantic love.

False love *"breeds in the emotion-thought of expectations, hopes, and conditioning . . . we expect that our relationship should make us feel good."* But she says that this *"dream collapses under pressure . . . such 'love' turns into hostility and argument."*

I interpret "pressure" as everyday, ordinary life, as well as crises.

False love, based on expectations and hopes, perfectly described my Bob period. It was never real, never honest or true. He had secrets – big ones. Not surprisingly it had turned into hostility and argument. Beck immediately gives the solution to this trajectory. When we just sit with our disappointment:

"Experiencing our pain . . . the melting of the false emotion can begin, and true compassion can emerge." (72/73)

Good relationships are about compassion, which is self-less instead of selfish. (It took a few years for me to *experience* compassion and thus to truly know it. I would discover that one of its components is empathy -- for a moment, being in the other's pain. I would also learn the difference between pain and suffering.)

With the exception of Rob's heart and my parent's deaths, to experience pain, to lean into pain, to acknowledge pain were all new to me. My solution to pain of any sort, whether emotional or physical, was to escape, or pretend it didn't exist -- denial -- or change my circumstances, never acknowledge it, particularly out loud. To acknowledge being hurt (or angry) was shameful to me. And I had many tactics for pain avoidance or denial: valium, shopping, movies, travel, comedy, and in an extreme, recent example, a new house in California.

Beck's solution was revolutionary to me. She urges us to stay with the suffering, *"go into the suffering and let it be."*

I believed that my ability to change unpleasant things, to make things better, for myself and others, was my great talent and my avenue to freedom. And sometimes this was true. But often I had only made things different, not better; and more of the same is

11

not better. Beck takes a very different tack regarding pain and freedom.

"Freedom is closely connected with our relationship to pain and suffering . . . Because of the fear of pain we all build up an ego structure to shield us, and so we suffer. Freedom is the willingness to risk being vulnerable to life; it is the experience of whatever arises in each moment, painful or pleasant." (189)

Her words are concise, simple. *"Freedom is . . . to risk **being vulnerable**."*

To *"risk being vulnerable"* was a scary endeavor for me. (Feminism was, and had formed, a shield of invulnerability for, and around, me.) Each morning I sat quietly, meditating, then reading and contemplating Beck's words. I began to understand the classic error I had made with Bob – I expected him to make me happy and fulfilled. I even expected him to help with my meditation – which is a solitary pursuit!

As Beck and countless therapists have pointed out, this is the original false premise of romance, at the base of many relationships. We erroneously expect our relationship "to be the one place that gives us peace." But they don't. Often they do the opposite, they make us miserable.

So, why have one at all? Why not go back to my alone state, the pre-Bob epoch? Beck immediately answers:

"We begin to see that they are our best way to grow. In them we can see what our mind, our body, our senses, and our thoughts really are . . . Why are relationships such excellent practice? Why do they help us to go into what we might call the slow death of the ego?" (88)

Because aside from meditation, *"there is no way that is superior to relationships in helping us see where we're stuck and what we're holding on to . . . So a relationship is a great gift, not because it makes us happy – it often doesn't – but because any intimate relationship, if we view it as practice, is the clearest mirror we can find." (89)*

This is what Marge Rock, my recovery therapist, had tried to tell me – a relationship was a mirror, an opportunity for self-awareness, an exercise for my ego to shrink; it was not simply about pleasure and security, it was about risk and vulnerability. It was not happily ever after at the movies, but a chance for self-insight and reflection.

Bob was a mirror – all the fear and withholding I saw in him were actually in me; my bottled-up anger was there, just below the surface. This was not at all what I imagined myself to be. And this fear, anger and righteousness, this crust of invincibility, had to surface in order to be removed.

"When a relationship isn't working, it means that the partners are preoccupied with 'I' . . . what I want."(96) Yes, this was true of Bob, always on the lookout for someone else. But it was also true of me.[8] I kept a mental list of what he *was not doing* for me, a list that grew longer each week.

"Our fear of our own annihilation leads to useless behaviors, including the effort to protect our self-image, our ego. Out of that need to protect comes anger. Out of anger comes conflict. And conflict destroys our relationships with others." (97)[9]

But in this instance, destroying the relationship was a very good thing. And that is a key point – if one is on a spiritual

13

path, wrong decisions will be righted, just as self-delusions will clear up.

Bob was a delusion, a bad choice. Just as I was for him. In spite of my clinging to the relationship, the universe intervened in the form of a Sufi massage therapist, to whom I will forever be grateful. And I was not annihilated, only a little humiliated, or maybe humbled. Once again, I was saved from my superficial choices in relationships – based on outer appearances rather than inner achievements.

My familiar emotional scenario --fear leading to ego protection and then on to anger and conflict and running away -- is a trajectory I will try to remember. I have taken this route so many times it has become ingrained, almost instinctual. The solution is counter-intuitive – when I fear self-annihilation (and the instinctual adrenaline of fight or flight), don't leave, don't argue, be still, be quiet, be strong.

For the first time in my **everyday** life,[10] I had consciously leaned into the pain rather than denying it or running away from it. I would be OK, no matter what happened. A mere *ten days* later, my speed dating experience erased any memory/thought of Bob. Seriously. Gone, in TEN DAYS! What a joy to regain sanity! And so quickly!

There were other gems in Beck's book that I stored in the back of my mind. I was unable to handle criticism, even contrary suggestions, from colleagues and dates.

"We feel that the only way to handle an attack is to fight back; and the way we fight is with our minds. We arm ourselves with our anger and our opinions, our self-righteousness." (**Everyday Zen**, 107)[11]

I lived in "I", the Great I or Me, on guard for disagreement and feminist injustice. As an intellectual and a smart woman with a great deal of concealed fear, I fought with my mind, armed with *opinions* and *self-righteousness*. My scholarly traits bled into my personal life. I cringe at the memories of my public academic arrogance. And I cringe today at what's left of my intellectual ego, and my lack of its awareness, in this book.

Like other Buddhist scholars, Beck cautions us against hope, suggesting that we choose life as it is, life without drama. Why? Aren't aspirations and hope important to essential, along with excitement? She would say *no* to both. They exist only in the future, and only in the mind. But even more importantly, they inflate the ego.

"No matter what our particular drama is, we are always at the center of it – which is where we want to be. Through practice, we gradually shift away from that self-pre-occupation . . . Thus, to move from a life of drama to a life of no drama, although it sounds extremely dull, is what Zen practice is about." **(Nothing Special**, 249)

For me, relationships were always high drama, which is why I stopped having them. They were painful, they hurt, and they were all about Me. But if I could be vulnerable and lean into the pain rather than defend my fearful ego against it, there was another way.

One brief Beckism completely reversed my thinking. I put it in my pocket, for quick retrieval. *"Sharp rocks are truly jewels."* (**Nothing Special**, 116) The metaphor would be echoed by Dr. Ashok Bedi, Jonathan's Indian psychoanalyst, *as the sand grit in the oyster that makes the pearl.* More of this, later.

Bob had served as great practice. The door to a relationship, which I had closed many years before, had been opened. Nine days later I met Jonathan.

At my sister Nancy's frustrated insistence, fed up with my moaning about being dumped, or *deep sixtied*, I called the recorded voice mails of men between 55 and 70 in the audio personals of the **Milwaukee Journal**. (This was 2001, the pre-dawn of Match.com and other online dating sites.) If the brief bios sounded interesting, I left my name and telephone number: "Hi, my name is Pat; I teach at the University, am tall and thin with streaked blonde hair. Oh, I love my books." Seriously. This is exactly what I said. Could I have been more idiotic? But they all called back the same day. How desperate is that!

From January 22 to 24, I speed dated, meeting six or seven potentials for afternoon coffee at the local Schwartz bookstores – an hour max. This experimental ego-booster would only be temporary until my desirability could be re-established or not. Then right back to the single life I had embraced and advocated to other women for so many years pre Bob blip. After all, who needed the pain and agony of dating? After the initial meeting, they all invited me on real dates. That was all the affirmation I needed. Without a second thought, I turned them down. I felt pretty terrific. I wasn't the drudge I imagined myself to be.

Now I could get on with my book on death and spirituality! The nightmare of Bob – failing to have a healthy relationship and then being dumped for a younger woman -- was over! except as comedy.

I didn't plan on *falling in love*, at sixty. But then I didn't count on meeting Jonathan in the coffee shop of Columbia

Hospital – which was adjacent to the University. I had stopped for coffee on my way to my last meeting, at 3:30, January 24, 2001. I was so over the desire to date that I didn't even "do" my hair or put on mascara that morning. But the energy in our initial encounter, and the conversation we had while he was waiting for the results of his thyroid exam (talk about high romance), were inspiring, thrilling.

He was 56, intelligent, attractive, **funny**, articulate, unconventional, even quirky, casually stylish in a Ralph Lauren way, and a *very* successful businessman, an entrepreneur who had become a professor at the university. After selling his trade publication company, a family company founded by his father, in 1994, he went to the renowned international business school, IMD in Switzerland as an executive in residence. He stayed for four years, at 55 receiving his PhD in family business. Now he was a Professor, teaching entrepreneurship in the Business School at the University of Wisconsin in Madison and writing his book on selling family companies.

I am embarrassed to write that I was *immediately* attracted to him. Few things have surprised me more than this – I didn't believe in love at first sight, just a romantic convention of the movies that I had analyzed in my 1996 book on women and film, **A Fine Romance: Five Ages of Film Feminism.** (My preferred title, refused by the publisher, was the clever **What Cinderella and Snow White Forgot to Tell Thelma and Louise**; it reveals my rather arch take on romance, couples and marriage**.)**

And if not unbelievable, then the encounter was ludicrous, maybe even lunacy. After all, I had just turned sixty! Sixty was hardly the age of loopy romance and exotic adventure. Particularly while reading Charlotte Beck's **Everyday Zen.**

When I told my daughter, Dae, in Manhattan, and my sister, Nancy, that "he could be the one," they thought I was in aftershock from the mysterious grand mal seizure I had in New York a month earlier, which had landed me in the emergency room of Presbyterian Hospital for Christmas Eve, unconscious again for several hours.

When I said I had agreed to visit him in Florida, where he had a condominium (I would stay in a nearby hotel), they both freaked! Was I nuts? Who was this guy? He could be a serial slayer of feminist professors. And he was a businessman, not a filmmaker or artist, my preferred choices. This behavior was nothing like me. What was I thinking?

Their alarm was sensible and logical. And not just for medical reasons. Or for using romance clichés like "he could be *the one*." But three weeks after this first encounter, I spent four days in New York, staying with Dae, and her husband, Larry, who waited up for me when I came back from my dates with Jonathan.

I confess to enjoying the luxurious way he traveled; I was honored by the way he was courting me -- with limousines and hotel suites and constant attention. And his desire for me, which he expressed enthusiastically, increased my interest in him. My deep seated fear of being abandoned (yes, I know, a much over-used cliché but still *true)* was soothed by his endearments and declarations of love.[12]

This man felt so familiar to me – our histories were so similar it was a bit uncanny. We went to the same college, worked at the same television station, WKOW in Madison, knew many of the same people, and now lived on the same street, Lake Drive, fourteen blocks apart, in Milwaukee. Our children had attended the same school, University School, and were of comparable ages.

18

Our fathers had the same birthday and sense of humor. It was as if we were old friends.

He was charming, a bit eccentric, offbeat and sophisticated, with a gregarious, playful personality. He was a mesmerizing story-teller and had a beguiling smile. Nothing daunted him; nothing was impossible; he took action effortlessly and perfectly. I loved his style, his energy. I was impressed by his self-confidence, and his competence -- the way he saw opportunity and took hold of life. I mentioned that I wanted to travel in Morocco. Less than two months later, there I was, in Morocco, in what was rapidly becoming a committed relationship.

After this *being sixty* incident in Morocco, repeated with therapeutic glee countless times by Jonathan at gatherings and parties (and chance encounters with strangers, whether store clerks or waiters -- "How old do you think she is?" -- he can be relentless in pursuit of the *good cause*), I gritted my teeth, held his hand, found my own extraordinary Jungian analyst in San Francisco, Dr. John Beebe – Jonathan had his Jungian analyst, Dr. Ashok Bedi -- and began to take another look at myself.

I went from rejection through acceptance and, I like to imagine, on to at least a small celebration of my 60 years. It took some time before I trusted his acceptance of my age. My interior visual critic was ruthless. Honesty became a premium, and a challenge, given my opening hedge about my age.

Jonathan was gregarious with all our guides and merchants, particularly the Moroccan rug hawkers, establishing short relationships with strangers who happily responded to his open, and amusing engagements. Jonathan was a character, a delightful, considerate, generous character.

The creativity of his competence and his tenacity will always amaze me. I had been used to doing everything myself – what a luxury it was to rely on another. Trust had been elusive for me. This feeling, which grew slowly in time, was one of comfort and relief, of relaxing after an exhausting journey.

But I suspect the quality that initially attracted me as much as any other, including his acumen as a businessman, was Jonathan's interest in my intellectual work – we talked about how my writing on theories of anxiety related to his work on selling family companies. My intellect didn't threaten him, rather, it fascinated him. In turn, I was equally entranced by his stories (and practices) of business – and understood how he had come to be successful and respected, without many of the pretensions that come with achievement and status.

At sixty, on January 24, 2001, at 2:30 p.m., my life took an abrupt turn, and within six months, I began to live a coupled life that I had fled in 1974 and to entertain thoughts of an institution, marriage, that I had disparaged for so long.

In retrospect, I think I was crying so uncontrollably in Morocco because I was afraid – I didn't know how to let my guard down, I didn't know how to maintain my independence and freedom with another, I didn't know how to risk being vulnerable. To be frank, I didn't know how to be completely honest and I knew little about my emotions.

Feminism made me stronger, but it had also made me arrogant and wary, if not downright suspicious, of men. Feminism gave me a focus and a career. It gave me a voice and a place in the academic world. It convinced me that my thoughts and my life and the lives of women mattered. It made me truly independent.

This relationship would made me stronger in a different way. It made me vulnerable, it humbled me, it taught me compassion. It showed me that I needed to learn how to truly listen, to be patient, acceptant, and unconditionally tolerant. The rest of this book is about the distance from that afternoon of shame and denial in Morocco, to being 60, or 70.

The Sea Ranch and The Buddha

In the fall of 2001, I took a year's sabbatical from the University and lived full time in my new house at Sea Ranch, California. I was, *yikes*, still 60. I had no job, no family, no friends, no *history* in the area to anchor me. For the first time in my life, I was without a built-in identity (as daughter, wife, or mother) or professional purpose. And there was no place to escape, no multiplex or mall. I had set the perfect scene for a life of simplicity and solitude. Now I had to live it.

Jonathan would fly out every weekend, from Madison, Wisconsin, where he was a Professor in the Business School, roaring up the Pacific Coast Highway 1 in his Porsche, making record time. His ardor captivated me: he missed only one weekend, when all the planes in the U.S were grounded – after 9/11/2001. (But I was not alone that historical day. Dae and Larry were visiting me from New York. The universe can be so mysterious in its affection.)

Three hours north of San Francisco, *The Sea Ranch* nestles along nine spectacular, windy miles of Northern California coastline, with its rugged bluffs, high surf, and cold seas. It is a dramatic locale, right out of the movies. The "planned" community was designed in the 1960s by architects who wanted to

21

"live lightly on the land," preserving an aesthetic balance between the built and the natural environments.

Simple modern houses of redwood or cedar, in subdued brown hues, are interspersed with nature preserves and walking trails. Soaring windows bring the outside in. The Design Committee approves every tree, window, or nail. You can imagine the drama of owners/builders. Property lines are not demarked, they merge and flow into each other. Landscape style is natural and indigenous. It cannot mark ownership.

Nature has not only provided a gorgeous backdrop, like living on a Hollywood movie set, but it also serves as a barrier to development, as does the isolation and lack of distraction. Sea Ranch is accessible only after an hour's drive along the ocean on the sharply curving Pacific Coast Highway, or the narrow, rough, steeply pitched Skaggs Spring Road through the mountains.

During the summer, a dense mist hovers over Sea Ranch like a protective covering for this enclave of 1500 houses and 500 permanent residents, many who left successful careers in their late 40s or early 50s to live here. Sometimes I think Sea Ranch is where over-achievers go to decompress before they die. Or where unrequited leaders can enact their unfulfilled professional desires as volunteers.

The nearby town of Gualala, population 685, also straddles Highway One. Along this short stretch, there are two supermarkets, two video stores, two lawyers, two gas stations, two hardware stores, one small gym, one local newspaper, the **Independent Coast Observer**, one drug store, several hotels, restaurants, art galleries and gift shops. Social interactions occur in the produce aisles at the Surf supermarket, at the P.O. Boxes, at Trink's Bakery or the funky Café LaLa, and at events in the

Gualala Art Center, built from redwoods by locals and full timers. Volunteers also refurbished the movie theater, thirty minutes north in Point Arena. Here, a bit bedraggled, the hippy 1960s are alive and well in clothing, hairstyle, and the drug culture, just barely underground and aging.

On the first day of my new life in a very small town, I did two things: I joined the gym, a small town social hub, and I attended the local meditation group. The bright little gym was a perfect place for an older stranger to go, without feeling too awkward. Fitness centers are public spaces in which one can be quiet, private. Yet the space affords the support and promise of human interaction. I had been lifting weights since the early 1980s, when the Nautilus centers were first built. (But I don't have anything near a taut body.) I had discovered that lifting weights was the best way to deal with my high anxiety. The after-sixty weight gain is another story.

Sea Ranchers are distinct from the "locals."[13] Elegant cuisine with paired wine courses is the favored entertainment. These lively dinner parties begin at 6 pm and end by 9 pm, an unwritten code. Our first time out, we pushed back our chairs after the dessert course, as did everyone else. We were settling in for after dinner conversation. Everyone else stood up, thanked the host and hostess, and left. We soon learned this was not eat and run, but local custom. In case a guest doesn't realize that the party is over at 9pm, one host will bring out the vacuum cleaner, or his bull horn, and make a public announcement.

Often retired and older *professionals*, some Sea Ranchers become amateur writers or painters, unless writing was one's real profession. Quilter is the most popular talent for Sea Ranch women who belong to quilting leagues; wood worker is the provenance for Sea Ranch men, formerly corporate leaders or successful entrepreneurs, who make beautiful bowls and furniture with expensive wood working tools in their enlarged garages. Still photographer is the third preferred talent, the result of treks into the Antarctic and other exotic journeys by retired couples, he photographing, she cataloguing and scrap booking; and amateur painting, watercolor and oil, appeals to both sexes.

Local galleries show these "emerging" artists, including quilters, now in their sixties and seventies and selling their work to their friends and neighbors. There are also serious and secretive hunters and gatherers – of mushrooms and huckleberries – who rarely shared their haunts. These pursuits didn't attract me, except art patron, at which I briefly excelled.[14]

Here, being a good neighbor and community volunteer, and being committed to environmental causes, are the highest values, with a coveted accolade, "Sea Rancher of the Year." Last year's winner is my AA sponsor.[15] I didn't really fit in but I loved being 60 here.

There was little pretense, makeup, or current fashion and much tolerance, a disdain of big egos, and a reverence for nature. This was just what I needed in my search for humility and contentment. And the local eccentrics added just a touch of spice and comfort to my everyday life.

My small town world now literally resembled that of Jessica Fletcher, in **Murder She Wrote,** her neighbors, an extended family, with the older generation the most influential, intelligent, and eccentric. The series was a celebration of Jessica's globe-trotting independence through her work as a bestselling author. In this dream of an active, productive old age, Jessica was always the best detective. She was not married and was dedicated to her work which made her a famous celebrity with influential friends around the world. In fact, Jessica had the best of both dreams of retirement -- she travels internationally **and** she lives in a Maine village (actually filmed in Mendocino, California) with a close-knit community of old, eccentric friends and neighbors who run the small, quirky town.

The program was about self-sufficiency, freedom, and the pleasures of work, with a critique of the younger generation along the way. Often marriages were a surface covering violence and hatred in families. The guest appearances of aging actors, familiar to us from their old films and TV series, resembled old friends at a college reunion, whom we recognized and then identified, connecting their aging bodies to their youthful selves. The increase in cosmetic surgeries on aging faces made recognition more difficult.

The irony that the coastal community of the series was actually on the west, not east, coast, in Mendocino, California, only one hour from my home in Sea Ranch, is not lost on me. Now I am retired, living on the coast, and writing a book, this book. I am trotting around the world, from Tibet to Manhattan, Nepal, and China; I am running into old friends along the way.

Sea Ranch is a small town, a community of fascinating, quirky neighbors, highly educated, kind and idiosyncratic in their own ways. Everyone knows everyone else. All the news comes in the weekly newspaper, the ICO, or is conveyed on the treadmills and stair machines in the gym. Being a neighbor and taking time for others is an art form. Unlike any other place I have lived, here I am watched over, cared for, and recognized as a neighbor. No wonder I loved this series. It prophesied my future.[16]

The meditation group, like AA, crossed all lines – of age, education, and economics. It met weekly for an hour at Mary Star of the Sea Catholic Church, on and around the altar. On my first visit, there were six or seven people sitting cross-legged in front of a burning candle. A humble gathering, nothing fancy.

I tiptoed in, as only a klutz can do, noisily arranged my big meditation cushion, which s*quished*, unfolded my several shawls, *swish swish,* wrapped myself up, took a deep breath, and tried to settle into meditation. This felt so good. A bell signaled the end of the forty-minute meditation. Wow! Time had vanished.

Then the others began reading from a book that they passed around. I joined in the circle, noticing the author's name, Charlotte "Joko" Beck, and the title, **Nothing Special**. (You already know about Joko Beck.) The words of the text were simple, clear. Just hearing them was uplifting. This was a Buddhist meditation group. Yet it felt completely familiar. I would attend sessions whenever I was in town.

Because northern California is filled with spiritual centers, many of the teachers would come to Gualala for weekend retreats. Most were Buddhist. So I began to learn about Buddhism – not to replace Gurumayi or Siddha Yoga but as knowledge to sit beside them. (The closest Siddha Yoga Center was 3 hours away, on curvy roads.) Buddhism, like Siddha Yoga, began in India, with the same roots and cultural traditions. What attracted me to these new texts, and there were many, was the joy I experienced when reading them – my soul was thirsty for this knowledge.

I try, and often fail, and then try again, to apply these insights to my everyday life. But old habits are hard to dislodge. I am willful and so emotional in my responses that this will take more time than I have. And compassion was not a first principle or priority in my western education as it is in Buddhism. But there is solace in the effort and wisdom in the intention.

Buddhism doesn't advocate what can be so off-putting to many about Western religions or Muslim and Hindu practices – the centrality of God or deities for attaining access to a spiritual or divine realm. (For AA members, God, particularly the Christian concept of God, is often the greatest stumbling block of the Twelve Steps. AA allays fear and difference by defining God as "a power greater than oneself," or adding, after "God," the words, "as we understand him." Venerable Henapola Gunaratana writes that:

"Buddhism's flavor is intensely clinical, more akin to psychology than religion. It is an ever-ongoing investigation of reality, of the very process of perception." Buddhism is a system, or a science, of the mind, "down to the very root of consciousness itself."[17]

Buddhism can be, therefore, very dense and complex. Older monks at the monasteries in Tibet are, in essence, studying for their PhDs. While there is much to learn in this 2600 year old tradition, it is also simple, for everyone, and to be used in everyday life.

There are many schools of Buddhism. But one thing is constant: Almost every book I read tells the founding story of Buddha's journey from the luxury and illusion of living in the palace as a prince to the reality of the world with illness, aging, and death. Eventually I realized that this could also be my story -- one of developing spiritual awareness of old age, sickness, and death and the freedom that can come from that awareness.

"Prince Shakyamuni [Buddha] was confronted with the inevitability of old age, sickness, and death," and he wondered why these were an *"inherent part of the human condition."*[18]

Although a young and wealthy man, he left the luxury of his palace and the kingdom and *"became a spiritual seeker in the traditional Indian way. He wanted to resolve the very reasons for birth, sickness, old age, and death."* So he lived the life of a wandering, penniless monk, begging, meditating and practicing rigorous asceticism. But his questions were not answered. He was emaciated but not enlightened.

He eventually gave up strict asceticism and advocated what he called "the middle way." He continued to meditate. Finally he realized that all things are just as they are, yet we are not aware of this. We concern ourselves with:

"Likes and dislikes, our gains and losses. (xi) But even with gains, we suffer because we fear losing the gain. We hold onto objects, experiences, feelings, and people with great attachment. Out of this attachment, we create separateness." Everything we *"experience as self and environment are temporary and constantly changing, and if we are attached to them they cause us suffering." (xii)*

I was holding on to so many things – particularly possessions; I could obsess over my losses on the stock market, never satisfied with my gains, which I would fear losing. In 1999, I bought a second house in California to be near to Rob but also as a place for the furniture I had inherited from my mother in 1997. I held on to old sad feelings of inadequacy, including a feeling of being separate from everyone. I couldn't shake my shame hang-over from my addiction, particularly the emotional harm I had caused Rob and Dae. Whenever they experienced any disappointments, fear, or doubts, I blamed myself. I was still attached and hence still fearful.

As I continued to rehearse my past offenses and failures, I created my own suffering . . . . in my brand new life, which had no remnants or reminders of my old and over past, except in my mind.

Buddha summarized what he had learned in the Four Noble Truths of Buddhism, one of his earliest teachings:

*"1) Suffering, 2) the cause of suffering, 3) the cessation of suffering, and 4) the path that leads to the extinction of suffering." "Suffering is unawareness of the impermanent nature of all things. We are in constant struggle, rejecting what we dislike and seeking what we desire." This "rejecting and seeking is the cause of suffering." (*Master Sheng-yen, xii)

Buddha (or Gotama, or Gautama, other names, from various countries, for Buddha) observed:

"As one craving after another took possession of his mind and heart, he noticed how human beings were ceaselessly yearning to become something else, go somewhere else, and acquire something they do not have. It is as though they were continually seeking a form of rebirth, a new kind of existence, even constantly changing our position, having a snack, talking to someone."[19] *(Armstrong 74/75)*

Recovering addicts recognize these cascading desires, which are never satiating, only endless. Beck calls them "emotion-thoughts" which we "fuss over." I could never do or be enough. I could never know enough, or publish enough or be recognized enough. My thoughts, not the reality of my life, were the cause of my suffering.

Buddha taught that suffering can be overcome, that if we realize the "fleeting nature of all things," suffering can be extinguished. The eightfold path is the way to do this.

"For his "forty-five year ministry, the Buddha taught all that was necessary to reach the goal of liberation." And he advised his disciples not to depend on him for leadership, but to "be islands unto your selves, refuges unto yourself."[20]

"For Gotama [Buddha], and others in India then, the prospect of living one life after another was horrifying." Today, many of us:

"Feel that our lives are too short and would love the chance to do it all again. But what preoccupied Gotama and his contemporaries was not so much the possibility of rebirth as the horror of re-death. It was bad enough to have to endure the process of becoming senile or chronically sick and undergoing a painful death once, but to be forced to go through all this again and again seemed intolerable and pointless." (Armstrong 9)

The simple logic is both true and liberating. There had to be another answer to existence, to the meaning of life.[21]

Buddha found it in the **Upanishads,**[22] which emerged shortly before his birth. A core teaching was that the highest, eternal reality was identical to one's own inner Self (Atman). (Armstrong, 25) This belief is also the foundation of Hindu variations, particularly Siddha Yoga, my personal practice. It eliminated the need for a priestly elite. Nirvana was to be *"found in the very heart of each person's being."* (Armstrong, 86)[23]

A memory changed Buddha's (Gotama's) spiritual quest – from one of rigorous austerities, what we might see as deprivation. He remembered a moment of bliss when he was a boy. It had come when he was sitting alone, in nature, and after he had felt the pain of other creatures. It was:

"A rapture which takes us outside the body and beyond the prism of our own egotism, unpremeditated joy, with nothing to do with craving and greed." "This surge of selfless empathy had brought him a moment of spiritual release." (67) "Had his teachers been wrong? Instead of torturing our reluctant selves, could we achieve enlightenment effortlessly and spontaneously?" (Armstrong, 68)

The answer is "yes," if we have tamed our restless mind and emotions. Compassion was the key. Sitting alone in the field, the young boy had experienced compassion.

Stephen Batchelor, a former monk in "both the Zen and Tibetan traditions," points out that the four *"truths of Buddha" are "not dogmas, simply beliefs. They must be experiences."* (5)[24] If they were only beliefs, it would be a religion, not a spiritual practice. He reiterates this point: *"The dharma is not something to believe in but something to do." (17)[25]*

This notion of lived, experienced thought, knowledge taken into action, is significant for me. There is an immense distance between what Batchelor calls "something to believe in" versus "something to do," between *intellectual* and *experiential* knowledge. I call the latter wisdom – when our thoughts, our actions, and our words are on the same track. Spiritual beliefs must be practiced in order to be known.

For Hinduism and Buddhism, perhaps for all spiritual beliefs, there is no path other than practice. I must confess that I believe in and have often professed meditation more than I have actually meditated; there can be a misfire among my thoughts, my words, and my actions. When my actions begin to speak louder than my words or beliefs, then I will be a true meditator.

Batchelor takes the Buddha's story and applies it to our everyday lives.[26]

"We too immure ourselves in the 'palaces' of what is familiar and secure. We too sense there is more to life than indulging desires and warding off fears . . . we realize that the only certainty in life is that it will end. We don't like the idea; we try to forget that too. . . Everyone collaborates in everyone else's forgetting . . . We seek to arrange the details of our world in such a way that we feel secure: surrounded by what we like, protected against what we dislike. Once our material existence is more or less in order, we may turn our attention to the psycho-management of our neuroses. Failing which, the worst anxieties can be kept at bay by a judicious use of drugs." (23)

But none of this works for long. Pain, illness, loss, and death keep returning in various forms.

"We still don't get what we want and still get what we don't want. . . . We may know this, but do we understand it?"

We cover it up, forget it, and return to the distractions of the world. *"For were we to understand it, even in a glimpse, it might change everything."* (23)

Although I have had intense experiences, and loved the tranquility that came with meditation, everything for me had not changed. My emotions could be roiled by my thoughts. Anger could best me by causing me to react unkindly. Self-pity and feminist injustice/aggression could turn my wonderful life into a sad tale of martyrdom. Although I knew that the problem came from my own mind, and was reflected in my roiled emotions, I looked for someone or something to blame.

Because we were together most of the time after 2002, Jonathan was often the perceived cause – by becoming irritated or angry or moody. When he felt attacked, he defended himself; then I felt attacked and I defended myself. Round and round. Attack/Defense, a very familiar worldly -- national and international -- dance. Or he was a tease – a brat, actually, who would continue to poke until he got a response. Ignoring him never worked, he continued until I eventually responded negatively and hence, for him, hurtfully. Then he would feel shame, and I would feel irritated by his depressed mood – and my irritation would trigger his ire – and around and around we would go -- all this from nothing! And about nothing! It (nothing) could be exhausting, it could escalate into a full-force blowup.

The key is that our dramas were about nothing -- *in the present*. But "n*othing*" was a deep well of **past** injuries and outmoded emotional responses, what Pema Chodron calls "reactive patterns," our "propensities." Which is why *nothing* was our biggest problem. *And one of which we initially had little awareness*. Not surprisingly, we could rarely remember what "nothing" was. Why? Because it truly **was** *nothing*.

(We would learn that self-awareness takes time, that it is an inside job. And like changing old habits, it takes tremendous work and discipline.)

This *nothing* solidified into a series of skirmishes. We might play tit for tat, matching point for counterpoint, or try to establish who did what first, or who did it the most or the loudest. The scenes could be initially playful, but the nothing could escalate into a ferocious storm, threatening to leave, and then walking out,[27] and always coming back, almost immediately.

How could words so affect me? I knew about *maya*, about the illusion of language. I had been on a spiritual path for years, what happened to my discipline? Where was the serene meditator? Where did all this shame come from? Why was Jonathan a shaming expert?

My relationship could be a sharp rock, indeed. When I defended my position, fortified with self-righteousness, I couldn't see the jewel of Joko Beck Or anything else except my distraught emotions. (Emotions can become a shield, shutting us off from the physicality of our surroundings.)

But when I listened, remained quiet, or stepped up right away when I was off key, my anger would melt, and I could see, with compassion rather than my lust for justice, the jewel that was *us,* or the jewel that was me, or at least the charm of the restaurant

I began to see that all my years of ardent spiritual practice had primarily been focused on my self-contained *actions* – initially the practices of meditating, chanting, and selfless service. I had worked on accepting others, on having no expectations or attachment to the outcome of my actions, overcoming my fears, including fear of public speaking by accepting frequent engagements; and letting go of my attachment to my children and to my parents. Although I had faced death, it is, after all, inevitable, neither a choice nor a personal failure. In certain ways, my practice had been all about Me -- granted a Me with higher aspirations.

Buddhism is all about *reactions* – and emotions – what Beck calls *emotion-thoughts*. It is a rigorous science through which we can train and discipline the mind, body, and spirit to literally see and react to the world and everything in it with equanimity and compassion rather than destructive emotions.

Like Siddha Yoga's "See God in each other," Buddhism importantly includes *you,* the *you* that comprises our mutual humanity and prevents us from being *separate*, a lonely state. And it took a relationship with Jonathan for me to begin to become aware of this – that *you* and *I* are one, and the same.

Eventually I would see the larger reason for this newfound knowledge – as an antidote to my self-sufficient way of living alone. Whenever I would experience upsetting emotions, I usually had them in private. Except for Rob and Dae, my emotions were secret, or so I imagined. When my old computer crashed, losing 200 pages of my book, **High Anxiety**, I completely freaked out – only my dogs BP and Baggins saw or heard the tirade. When my father had criticized me as I drove him to the hospital for his regular blood transfusions, I could wallow in self-pity, but no one would know.

I could be irritable, I could be angry and hurt – without consequences. My reactions (and pride) belonged mainly to me. As long as I lived alone, the shame of experiencing what I believed to be negative emotions, particularly rejection, hurt, and anger, was manageable. Only my daughter, on the telephone in New York, could hear through my pretense.

But when I began a 24/7 relationship, Jonathan would react to my reactions – sometimes with irritation or hurt. And given his narcissistic bent, he took most things personally. Initially his responses bewildered me – I was just talking to myself out loud (which I had been doing for fifteen years! thank you very much!) Or, I'm allowed to express my feelings towards inanimate objects like my computer, aren't I? Or I would deny my emotions, pretending they didn't exist. **No! Of course not! I'm not angry!**

But he saw through my denials of hurt or anger. He would accuse me of being "inauthentic," which made him even more upset. It was initially so infuriating to have no private space for excess or negative emotions. **"Yes, I'm furious but it will pass if we ignore it**," just wouldn't cut it with him.

To be honest, I often didn't know what emotion I was feeling other than he was over-reacting and I was being treated unjustly, unfairly. And because I viewed these emotions as illegitimate, base feelings, I couldn't acknowledge them, at least out loud. But I did know how to childishly act them out.

The minefields of emotions that would play out caught me by surprise. I regularly packed my bags and left, dragging my little, reluctant dog, Rishi, after me. But I always came back, sometimes minutes later. I didn't want to leave him, I just wanted to escape my own skin, my own shame at being less than noble or kind or tolerant or perfect.

I hated failing. I couldn't deal with criticism. And he judged, everything, alas, as a matter of course. I couldn't withstand another's anger at me. I still fear anger, even of strangers. And Jonathan's hurt was expressed as anger, which he had in abundance. And I was an easy and willing target because I still carried interior shame – Jonathan had talent for shaming via endless repetition of my offenses.

Or Jonathan would come after me. Which is what I wanted and needed – reassurance that he did love me, that he was at fault, not me. I hated being wrong and being the bad guy. How could the martyr be wrong, or the villain? So much sound and fury and raw pain coming from within me. And from within him. Our pasts could be very heavy. Where did this anger and hurt come from? Where had it been hiding all these years?

It took two of the finest Jungian psychoanalysts, Dr. John Beebe in San Francisco, and Dr. Ashok Bedi in Milwaukee, to **explain** these destructive emotions. Dr. Ashok Bedi, Jonathan's Indian psychoanalyst -- who has infused Jungian principles with Eastern spiritual philosophy -- has a metaphor for the irritants and conflicts in relationships. He sees them as the sand grit in the oyster that ultimately creates the pearl.

For him, these grating frictions – replays and mutations of age-old complexes -- can be beneficial if not transforming. All we need for old pain to turn into joy is to develop the *awareness* of these unconscious patterns of thought.

Sound easy? Not at all! Because they are old and deeply buried and we are unaware of their nature, this is clearly not a simple task. Which is where a psychoanalyst comes in – as the translator of flailing emotions into their underlying causes and subsequent patterns of behavior. An intimate relationship can thus become a means of self-healing by uncovering and then taming old fears and insecurities.

Now this is easier said than done. Going through old defenses or complexes involves pain, it takes staying power, to say nothing of humility and surrender. To say that these are not my strong points is a severe understatement.

Early on, Dr. Bedi told us there were two kinds of relationships – the *horizontal*, which stayed on the surface, smooth, without either waves or storms or tsunamis, or *vertical*, which meant going deep, truly getting to know another. One involved pain and work, the other didn't. Of course, as two big egos, we chose the challenging course – the vertical, going deep.

As I have repeated perhaps too many times, Jonathan and I both brought old baggage into our new partnership. Neither of us initially had much awareness of the effect our fears and defenses had on the other. We were both too enthralled with our own stories, or blinded by our own pain, or caught up in our own fears, or seeking praise and credit for our actions while denying any blame.

In addition, I had no role models for intimate relationships. When taken individually, my parents were gracious, intelligent, generous people – beloved by their children, many friends and extended family. And they truly loved and were devoted to each other.

But the way they often conducted their marriage was another story, particularly for young children. First would come a small criticism (Peg, the beans are burned again, or Bob, you need to watch your weight); then bickering, which would erupt with my father's shouting, door slamming walk-out, and my mother's tears in the closest bathroom. These scenes never changed – they simply replayed. They were food fights.

My own marriage, now more than a quarter of a century ago, locked in my fear of long-term commitment. It went something like this: I would become dependent and trapped in his limited ambition and achievement, embalmed in a stifling boredom and inequality, with no financial independence or security.

As a result of this fear of entrapment, akin to being buried alive, my solution to disagreements and squabbles is to leave, or at least threaten to leave. The internal pressure to run away builds to such an intolerable degree that I feel as if I will implode. Instead, I explode – and say things I regret, necessitating apologies and the attendant quilt. Our mutual explosions felt more like mortar fire than sand grit.

As Dr. John Beebe, my Jungian psychoanalyst in San Francisco, says, we don't have complexes; rather our complexes have us.

Jungian psychoanalysis, my fourth amateur knowledge (after AA, Siddha Yoga, and Buddhism), is remarkably compatible with Buddhist (and Hindu) philosophy, particularly regarding the stages of life and the value of old age as a time of spiritual endeavor. (Dr. Ashok Bedi, Jonathan's psychoanalyst who came from a lineage of Indian gurus, or teachers, has entwined these two systems, enriching one by elaborating the other.[28]) But I must confess that I was not drawn to reading Jung as I had previously been to Freud. His prose was dense and my brain was tired of working so hard. So my knowledge is secondary and cursory, just enough to make sense of my analyst's commentary on my life.[29]

Carl Jung, the loyal disciple and heir of Freud, broke with him in 1913. The reasons were personal and intellectual. Jungian analysis was developing substantial differences from Freudian,[30] including the role of the analyst, which Jung saw as involved and participatory. Rather than seeing symptoms as a "form of futile suffering," Jung saw them as "an invaluable opportunity to become conscious and to grow." Symptoms were the *"growing pains of a soul struggling to escape fear and find fulfillment."* (125)

Dr. Bedi greeted each repeated sad tale of our conflicts with a joyous "Wonderful! This is great! Your souls are involved in a dance with each other. Do you want my feedback?" Unfailingly, this was always his positive response to dark moods and anguished voices and dramas. It was hard to hold onto feelings of tragic, hopeless, woe is me injustice in the face of such authoritative, intelligent optimism. Dr. John Beebe, my shrink, took our ragged scenes as clashes between our *types* which he would then unravel, like an intuitive magician.

For Dr. Bedi as for Jung, *"Pain is a valuable spur to self-examination, an incentive to 'wake-up'."* The Jungian analyst "encourages the patient to participate in his suffering," to "confront its meaning and mobilize the healing power of the unconscious." (128) Which sounds remarkably similar to Buddhist teachings, not surprising given Jung's fascination with Eastern philosophy, including the *I Ching*. Jung had a deep spiritual (not religious) bent and believed that *"the more secular, materialistic, and compulsively extraverted our civilization became, the greater the unhappiness."* (129)

Jungian analysis encourages us to accept "full responsibility for our circumstances." (128) Each of our therapists traced problems and solutions back to their respective client. As a result, I loved joint sessions with Dr. Bedi, and Jonathan loved sessions with my therapist, Dr. Beebe. Jonathan would be amazed that he "would get off so easily," for something he had initiated. Or that I would not retaliate against Beebe's admonitions. True, I would try to hedge and wiggle out of accepting full responsibility, always seeking qualifications and offering explanations. But blame, like partial responsibility, just wouldn't fly with either therapist. "The real therapy only begins when the patient sees that it is no longer father and mother who are standing in [her] way, but [herself.]" (131)[31]

While Freud looked backward, often to infantile sexuality as a cause, "Jung's tendency was to look forward," to goals. Not surprisingly, given his recurring and painful cancer of the mouth and use of cocaine and morphine, Freud feared old age. For Jung, old age is a continuation of our development. He called this lifelong process *individuation* – a confrontation "between the conscious subject who experienced and struggled to survive, and the unconscious 'other,' in the personalities and powers that forced themselves on him." (38) This "heightened consciousness" of what was unconscious sounds similar to the Buddhist notion of "awareness."

When he was 82, Jung wrote that:

"The only events of my life worth telling are those when the imperishable world erupted into this transitory one . . . All other memories of travels, people . . . have paled beside these interior happenings."(43)

The thing about death that impressed Jung the most was: *"the lack of fuss the unconscious makes of it. Death seemed to him to be a goal in itself, something to be welcomed."* (45)

While this is diametrically different from Freud, who feared death, it is also different from Buddhism. Whereas Jung's ultimate question was whether we are related to something infinite or not, for Buddhists the answer could only be affirmative, if they even asked the question. (42)

In 1921, Jung published **Psychological Types** – an area of his complex, varied theory in which my analyst, Dr. John Beebe, is a noted authority.[32] Jung's types refer to the way we perceive and respond to reality and how "people differ in using the four components." (85)[33] My analysis deals with the collision and interplay between Jonathan's and my types.

Beebe tells me that I am an *extroverted intuitive,* and that Jonathan is an *introverted feeling* type – that we are diametrically oppositional. If I can understand his type, "I will have the keys to the kingdom," and there is nothing I will not be able to grasp. Our opposition continues in what Jung calls *auxiliary* functions. *Thinking* is my *auxiliary function* and s*ensation* (dealing with the logistics of the outer world) is my *inferior function,* my real weak spot. Jonathan's is *thinking.* And *sensation* is his auxiliary function.

But the good news is that because of our typologies, we are also predictable. Hence, our squabbles can be dissected by an authority versed in Jung's types. Ergo, Dr. John Beebe. The intellectual explanation of what triggers pain and conflict causes both to disperse, like popping bubbles or balloons. Amazing! So I understood intellectually what was going on, but I still didn't know how to change.

For four years, we regularly called Beebe and Bedi every week, sometimes adding joint-emergency telephone sessions, CPR interventions to resuscitate a momentarily drowning relationship, huddling around one of our cell phones on speaker, shouting our various complexes ("Can you hear me?"), detailing personal arguments ("Are you still there?"), while walking through some airport, or freeway gas station ("Hello, Dr. Bedi/Beebe"), or riding in cabs, never noticing how strange this must have seemed to our drivers or passersby, hearing intimate details declared in public space, with no awareness of being overheard. ("Yes, Dr. Beebe, Jonathan's mother complex."). Emotionally distressed and sometimes furious, we competed for the status of injured party, both wanting to be right, or to receive credit, and oblivious to everything except the need to resolve our misunderstanding and our respective pain.

In retrospect, like all of our arguments and scenes, these are very, very funny. All about *nothing* . . . except the will to be right, which is a very destructive *something.* We gathered evidence, marshalling proof – whack, whack.

Very gradually, with the weekly guidance of two psychotherapists, but particularly with the wisdom of Pema Chodron and Ayya Khema and the many other Buddhist teachers whose books I was reading, and the collaboration of Jonathan, I began to gain awareness of and take responsibility for my old habits and reactions – for the emotions both decorous and furious they unleashed and then unloaded on others.[34]

Gradually I am defusing their old familial sources and patterns – particularly my intense response to anger or rebuke from men, a fear response locked in during my childhood with a very good father who also, and often, yelled, slammed doors, and stormed out. As these reactions are being slowly tamed, I am changing, at last.

For me, the key is my reaction, my response – I can be compassionate and truly listen with patience or I can feel hurt, feeling second best. I can consider Jonathan's emotions –

expressed even in cruel ways -- seriously, or I can judge them, usually as excessive or ridiculous or in need of atomic retaliation.

In choosing compassion, I treat myself with tenderness as well as Jonathan. Patience allows time to listen or time to cool down. When I react by choosing anger, I make both of us miserable. Mmmmm . . . let's see, which one? Oh, compassion, yes.

If the positive choice is so obvious (and so easy -- silence and listening), then why is it so difficult?

I have more than 50 years defending myself against or repressing emotions I didn't understand or like but emotions which I also learned -- my father's sudden anger and irritability, my mother's martyrdom. I thought they were reactions to reality. That reality needed to change, not me. When I chose compassion, my higher self emerged. But more often, my ego, my false pride, took over and defended itself. The scenario of the martyr emerges, triggering the need to run away – which my father and mother both did, usually getting only as far as the garage (my dad) and bathroom (my mother).

The moment of choice is subtle, and short, but this space between thoughts and words is always there. What to do? Run away? Be righteous, or simply right? Or stay, which means experiencing pain, learning about surrender as strength and humility. Do I want to polish this pearl, or do I want to find another oyster without so much history? No matter – the same insecurities will come up in me. And if it's not an ex-wife or dead mother who can become prominent in another's imaginary, as is the case with Jonathan, there will be something else.

If I can stay, if I can listen, if I can surrender my will to be righteous or even right, then we can go somewhere beyond our personal fears and limitations. Of course, there is a third option – becoming an oyster myself, without either the sand grit or the pearl. This will leave me without the friction. But then I will lose the insight that the frictions can reveal.

For me, along with Gurumayi Chidvilasananda, my Guru, the American Buddhist nun, Pema Chodron, has the answers. This brilliant woman was trained in the Tibetan tradition of Buddhism, as a student of Chogyam Trungpa Rinpoche, a meditation master who founded Naropa University in Boulder, Colorado.[35] I have learned much from three of her books, **The Wisdom of No Escape**, **When Things Fall Apart**,[36] and **The Places that Scare You**.[37] (Later on, I would take three retreats with her in California, along with online courses and reading her more recent works.)

I cannot improve on her words, which are honed to perfection via her personal experience and years of arduous practice, so the quotations will be lengthy. We need to:

"Face how we harm others, and it takes a while . . . because of mindfulness, we see our desires and our aggression, our jealousy and our ignorance. We don't act on them; we just see them. Without mindfulness, we don't see them. . .The next step is refraining . . . It's the quality of not grabbing for entertainment the minute we feel a slight edge of boredom coming on. It's the practice of not immediately filling up space just because there's a gap. . . If we immediately entertain ourselves by talking, by acting, by thinking – if there's never any pause – we will never be able to relax. We will always be speeding through our lives." (WTFA, 33)

"We learn to pause for a moment . . . it's a transformative experience to simply pause instead of immediately filling up the space. By waiting, we begin to connect with our fundamental restlessness as well as fundamental spaciousness." (35/36)

"Buddhism teaches that there are four things that we like and become attached to and four things that we don't like and try to avoid . . . First, we like pleasure; we are attached to it. Conversely, we don't like pain. Second, we like and are attached to praise. We try to avoid criticism and blame. Third, we like and are attached to fame. We dislike and try to avoid disgrace. Finally, we are attached to gain, to getting what we want. We don't like losing what we have." **Becoming immersed in "these four pairs of opposites – pleasure and pain, loss and gain, fame and disgrace, and praise and blame – is what keeps us stuck in the pain of samsara, the world." (46)**

"We carry around a subjective reality, which is continually triggering our emotional reactions. Someone says 'You are old,' and we enter into a particular state of mind, either happy or sad, delighted or angry . . . the irony is that we make up these eight worldly dharmas. We make them up in reaction to what happens to us in this world. They are nothing concrete in themselves." (47)

"We might feel that somehow we should try to eradicate these feelings . . . A more practical approach would be to get to know them . . . to see that they aren't all that solid . . Then the eight worldly dharmas become the means for growing wise as well as kinder and more content."

"Seeking security or perfection, feeling self-contained and comfortable, is some kind of death . . . We are killing the moment by controlling our experience." Chodron advises us to sit on the

razor's edge, not hanging on to being right or wrong, being in that space where "we're not entirely certain about who's right and who's wrong. . . Could we have no agenda when we walk into a room with another person, not know what to say?" Everything is ambiguous, everything is always shifting and changing. (83)

"We think that by protecting ourselves from suffering, we are being kind to ourselves. The truth is, we only become more fearful, more hardened, and more alienated. We experience ourselves as being separate from the whole. This separateness becomes like a prison for us, a prison that restricts." (87) "When we protect ourselves so we won't feel pain, that protection becomes like armor that imprisons the softness of the heart . . . When we breathe in pain, somehow it penetrates that armor." (89)

*"The journey goes down, not up . . . Instead of transcending the suffering of all creatures, we move toward the turbulence and doubt. We jump into it. We tiptoe into it . . . We explore the reality and unpredictability of insecurity and pain, and we try not to push it away." (**When Things Fall Apart**, 92)*

When I can *"explore the reality of insecurity and pain,"* I become aware of the mirror a relationship can be. I can see myself in him; and I can see myself through his eyes. Both views are ultimately generous and acceptant – of sags, wrinkles, flaws, quirks, habits, pains and all the imperfections that make us human.

"The painful thing is that when we buy into disapproval, we are practicing disapproval. When we buy into harshness, we are practicing harshness . . . The more we do it, the stronger these qualities become. How sad it is that we become so expert at causing harm to ourselves and others. The trick then is to practice gentleness and letting go . . . Instead of struggling against the force of confusion, we could meet it and relax. We can learn to

meet whatever arises with curiosity and not make it such a big deal." (27)

      I am trying to apply this scrim, which I learned from Gurumayi, to my words: Are they necessary? Are they honest? Are they kind? Many of my little remarks are not, at core, kind. My irony can slip into deep sarcasm. In **Be An Island,** Khema stresses the right time for speaking.

      "The right time to speak is when we are completely calm and the other person is attentive, at ease, and ready to listen. If there's anger, it's the wrong time. . . Unless we learn these skills, we will have many emotional accidents in our relationships."

I love this phrase, "emotional accidents." Most importantly, I am learning to hold my ground, as Buddhism teaches, to admit my responsibility, to accept criticism and then to own the error. Interior pain is unfailingly a sign that I am learning about surrender, patience, and humility – the triad that makes unconditional love possible. As feminism had done for me previously, helping me discern the way women were viewed and contained in the real world as well as on television and in the movies, an intimate relationship is leading to self-awareness.

      AA encourages us to take personal inventory, a detailed analysis of our "character defects." Some of my defects had not been glaringly apparent as long as I lived alone. Or at least so I imagined. But there was no one there to tell me. Being in a relationship was a different story, with a great deal of feedback. I had much to learn.

      Ayya Khema points to many of them in **Be an Island:**

"Creating our own viewpoint is one of the worst errors we make when we believe we are listening . . . Listening means being empty of self-importance and reacting to what we hear with empathy . . . Just listening, with total attention . . . without making up our own story about it, without our mental chatter, is part of compassion. It is also loving kindness." (48)

"In war there is never a winner, only losers . . . both sides lose. The same applies to a feeling of being victorious, of being the one who knows better or who is stronger or cleverer. Battle and peace do not go well together." (62)

Just so in relationships. There are only losers when emotions go into competitive battle.

"Is it really peace we want? Or do we want to be somebody special, somebody important or lovable? A somebody never has peace." (63) "Wanting to be somebody is dangerous . . . it hurts constantly." (64)

I think I wanted to *"be somebody"* even with this book, including being somebody by knowing Gurumayi.

"Being content means being satisfied with what we own and with how we look, speak, live, and react." (94)

I have some distance to go but I am on my way.

I had not been able to do this alone. It took a partner who wanted what he calls "emotional intimacy." This also meant *practicing* the principles of Buddhism (and Siddha Yoga) in my everyday ordinary life instead of simply *enjoying* them in my books and thoughts and applying them to life or death issues. (There is physical pleasure in reading books about spirituality, a soothing, enriching intellectual delight which can become a substitute for *practicing* spirituality.)

As the American Buddhist scholar, Robert Thurman, tells us,[38] the key to all the various schools of Buddhism is:

"The realization of the Buddha's teaching is not an intellectual or philosophical pursuit . . . it must be put into practice in daily life. . . Only in this way can it free us from the fetters of disturbing emotional afflictions and suffering, and enable us to realize enlightenment."

"The enlightenment of the Buddha was not primarily a religious discovery. It was not a mystical encounter with 'God' or a god . . .The Buddha's enlightenment was rather a human being's direct, exact, and comprehensive experience of the nature and structure of reality. . . 'Buddha' is not a personal name; it is a title, meaning 'awakened,' 'enlightened.'" (9)[39]

Similarly to Siddha Yoga, any of us can attain enlightenment, or Buddhahood. And we can do it in this lifetime, not after death, in some other place, but right here and now, no matter who we are, or what we have done, no matter how smart we are or are not. It is there for everyone – if we can see it.[40]

With the Buddhist meditation group as my touchstone, I spent the fall semester in Sea Ranch trying, and usually failing, to write this book. I had an alliterative title, *On Death and Dating,* but I had little to say about the latter.

We were very busy just being together and becoming a couple. And very restless. He loved great hotels, and I loved the adventure of new places. We both enjoyed being with our children, now doubled for each of us. We wandered from place to place, sometimes productively, always enjoyably.

In December of 2001, Jonathan arranged for us to spend two weeks on the CEO fast track of the Mayo Clinics – in Jacksonville, Florida and Rochester, Minnesota -- seeking a diagnosis for my mysterious grand mal seizures. During my four-day "fasting" test, he settled into a corner of my hospital room, nesting, creating a miniature office complete with computer, printer, and hanging files. He loved "playing office," his favorite game as a child, and served as a gracious host to the battalion of specialists who were trying to diagnose the source of my ailment.

The team of doctors concluded that rather than epilepsy, I had a rare pancreas disorder – producing an excess of insulin that would devour my blood sugar, precipitating grand mal seizures. They strongly recommended surgery to remove a section of my pancreas; after consulting with Rob (who had gone to medical school) and Dae, the smartest woman I know, I declined. I knew about the pain and risks of abdominal surgery from a 1982 near death experience and six weeks in the hospital. I would be careful about my diet. And the disease has abated, at least when I don't have too much sugar or white flour.

In October, we had visited Hawaii to meet Jonathan's parents, George and Dorothy, and his brother, and sister-in-law, Dave and Kathleen, from whom he had been estranged. The welcome we received from this witty and loving foursome was generous beyond my imagination. This began a joyous process of reconciliation and healing.

It started with a simple question I asked Jonathan. "What do you want? A loving relationship with your brother or do you want to be right?" He picked love and stuck to it (with a few small relapses of defensive righteousness). The reconciliation was fostered by his parents' acceptance of the past and of me, and Dave and Kathleen's graciousness and hospitality. They included us in their social events, along with hosting fabulous parties, and making us feel completely at home. Bygones became just that. I loved them all, and I will never forget their loving acceptance of me. We visited Honolulu every other month.

In January of 2002, after renting a home in Kailua for six weeks, we almost bought a house and moved to Oahu. Fortunately (or not), our bid on a beach house in Kailua was not accepted. After Jonathan's mild heart attack in Honolulu, we returned to Silicon Valley and bought a condominium in Menlo Park, near Stanford University's medical center, 3½ hours from Sea Ranch. We found superb specialists for our respective medical problems – Jonathan loved Rob's cardiologist. And we knew we had found the perfect climate and setting for our old age – Northern California.

Now we each owned a house in California – hedging our bets in case things didn't work out. We lived together, economically separate but equal. That summer of 2002, wanting to live fulltime in California, not Wisconsin, I retired from the University, sold my condominium in Milwaukee, and moved everything to my home in Sea Ranch. To be honest, Jonathan and his brother Dave, with great perception, called me on my fear of relationships, forcing an outcome. I made the decision to leave the University and my hard-earned, rather plush job and status quickly, so that I would not change my mind. Commitment still terrified me, being equated with imprisonment as it had been for so many years.

Meanwhile, Jonathan had given his wife all the personal property in his divorce. And he had given up more than one-half of his wealth, no small sum. The divorce was emotionally messy, expensive, with vitriol to spare. Although he had few personal possessions, Jonathan hauled truckloads of "business" to his new office in Gualala, California. He also kept his movie size popcorn popper, the first prop for our home movie theater. We began the process of remodeling and redecorating two houses, with two talented gay decorators – no small task and sometimes a tense one.

Jonathan's mind worked deductively; mine was strictly inductive. Jonathan worked through a step by step, logical process, I used intuition and randomness. That I would begin before I had a plan for the whole drove him nuts. So did my making mistakes and then returning them to the store. He began to think I had a distribution business. To me, he spent too much time talking and meeting. I wanted to get on with it!

Impatient (and judgmental) as I was, I always trusted his sense of style; he has superb taste and is highly creative. My indecisiveness loved deferring the final choice to him. In these instances, his judgments served me very well. Eventually, I would realize the great value of his commentary, what Dr. Beebe would call "the eyes in the back of my head."

Paradoxically, although retired, life was busier. Our respective constituencies had doubled. Between us, there were two parents, four adult children, four in-laws, two siblings, Dave and Nancy, along with Kathleen, and, since 2002, three beautiful granddaughters: Remi, Siena, and Alessandra. Regular travels to Denver, where Jonathan's son, David, lived, and Tulsa, where his daughter, Amy, had just moved, began to heal old familial wounds.

We regularly spent time in New York with Dae and Larry, who loved and admired Jonathan. He would become their business mentor. Rob immediately liked and respected him, and would come to love him. Amy would warm up to me eventually, but this took some painful time for both of us. She is an extraordinary woman, teacher, and mother.

Jonathan and I were buddies, we were partners, we hung out, we made new friends, and we traveled – together, often for 24/7.[41] Our days began with coffee, **The New York Times,** and morning talks in bed; they ended with books in bed. We read sections to each other, sharing thoughts and encounters from the day. We wrote together, we went to movies, plays, AA meetings, and lectures together, we decorated two houses together, we spent time with our adult children together, and we cared for our granddaughters together. Jonathan was infinitely more patient than I was; he loved child play and general goofiness. I loved the girls and looked forward to their growing independence and conversation. We all loved Disney cruises in the middle of winter.[42]

Sea Ranch is about the present – in California, with new friends, and without a career and the identity that had accrued from thirty years as a Professor. At 60 my life abruptly shifted directions, allowing me to go back and clear up old interior wounds, along with granting me companionship, adventure, and intimacy. Being 60 is about aging and acceptance, of another and of myself; like motherhood, it is about unconditional love for Jonathan and myself. And it is about the sheer *pain* that comes with change – the change that it takes to truly *accept* myself and another. This pain is a step on the way to joy and freedom, this pain, if acknowledged and endured, transforms into gratitude.[43]

This is Charlotte Beck's sharp rocks; and it is also the passionate anguish the Sufi poet-scholar Rumi wrote about. Acknowledging, embracing, or leaning into pain is a key to

Eastern traditions of meditation and philosophy. This is a far cry from the Western pursuit of pain avoidance and the denial of death that drives consumer/drug culture and most of our lives.

For years, I tried to build up my ego, only to learn that it was also the source of my fear and anxiety. Solution: turn around, face it, and walk through fear rather than run away from it. This can be like a walk through fire, only to discover at the end that the fire didn't burn, it was only burning in my mind.

Being Nobody Going Nowhere, like **Nothing Special**, is a perfect title for this process.[44] The sense of ego is miniscule, humble. The author, Ayya Khema, was German-Jewish and lived through the Second World War.[45] Afterward, she became a Buddhist nun and founded a Theravada monastery in Australia, despite the fact that this tradition "denied her full ordination." She became an activist, founding several Buddhist centers in Sri Lanka and Germany, and teaching around the world, including California, until her death in 1997.[46]

Khema describes one persistent pattern of my life:

"In daily living, we try to get rid of unpleasant feelings by getting rid of the people who trigger them in us, by trying to get rid of situations, by blaming others instead of looking at the feeling . . . This reaction of ours, trying to keep the pleasant and trying to get rid of the unpleasant, is a circular movement . . . It doesn't have a doorway . . . [it is] a never-ending circle. The only opening leading out . . . is to look at the feeling and not to react." (31)

Not react? Not defend the injustice of it all? Not blame my parents, my economic circumstances, my former husband, my job, or even child rearing? Or find an escape hatch or clause out of a painful situation? Or hedge the truth? Deny? Cry? How would *not reacting* be possible?

I have left so many relationships behind, I have run away from so many skirmishes with people – I got rid of, or iced, people who triggered any unpleasant thoughts. Rarely did I ever "look at the feeling." I used to take valium to avoid any "unpleasant feelings." (32) And thus, in one "situation" after another, I repeated the same behavior, trapped in a circular logic.

Khema's solution is so simple, so easy, and it doesn't cost anything. (Initially, it can hurt.) Khema suggests: *"There's no one to blame for the feelings that arise. These are just feelings that arise and cease."*

I love the comfort of "just feelings," without the emotional charge, without the negative punch, without the high drama and shame.

"Watch the feeling and know. Unless you stand back and look at an unpleasant feeling and not dislike it you will never be able to effect a change." Our mind will be like *"a muddy driveway on which the car goes back and forth and the ruts get deeper and deeper. . . When we see that we don't need to pay any attention to our thoughts, it becomes easier to drop them. When we see that we don't have to react to feelings, it is much easier to drop the reaction."* (33)

I don't need to "pay attention to my thoughts?" I will not die from my feelings? Where did I get the idea that **not** to react was subservience, timidity, or even passive aggression? And that to flare up in a ready retort or defense or justification was a sign of courage and openness? Just "drop the reaction?" A sweet command indeed. But for me, with ingrained habits trained like Pavlov's dog, no small task.

My solution to painful feelings was to have an emotional meltdown and then escape, which sometimes took the form of shopping. I simply covered up or replaced one feeling with another. These quick fixes never lasted. Why? The causes of human problems are: *"wanting pleasurable sensations, wanting the gratification, often not getting them and never being able to keep them."* The first step of letting go of wanting is:

To sit with an uncomfortable sensation. Not wriggling and shifting around, not trying to get out of this discomfort by changing position. There is no wriggling out of suffering. Suffering cannot be eliminated in this way. The only out of it is to let go of craving. One can't wriggle out of craving. One really has to let go it." (60)

We can practice not wiggling out of suffering in meditation. The discomfort in our sitting positions *"gives us a wonderful opportunity to learn about our sensual desires . . . One leg will hurt, I move, then the next leg cramps, I shift direction . . . etc. Or one entertainment finishes, boredom sets in, I want another. It's a lost cause."* (61)

Being in a "serious relationship" (many steps above "dating"), which is where I now found myself, was the last thing I would have imagined for my future as an old woman. My future would be living alone or in an ashram. And these are noble choices for those who already know how to have close, intimate relationships. I didn't. Nor did I know much about real tolerance and vulnerability.

In addition, my deep-seated belief in my own inadequacy and unattractiveness were dark notions that needed to surface in order to be removed. It took a relationship to do this. Now this might sound paradoxical, to say nothing of masochistic. Perhaps. But it is also about experiencing and unraveling the mystery of many women's lives – how to truly love another and not give yourself away – that I have spent my professional life analyzing in film and on TV, and in my personal life escaping.

Initially, I had two ingrained obstacles to overcome – obstacles which I saw as achievements. I think they might be typical of women of my generation, women who were young in the 1950s and 1960s.

The struggle for me has been to become the author of my own life. I wanted to write my own script, as well as being the lead and directing the show. I was not comfortable as a supporting character, I liked center stage. (And when I had it, I also feared it and often didn't know what to do with it.) Maybe that's why I admired and wrote about "*I Love Lucy.*" And other strong women who took center stage – Katherine Hepburn, Jane Fonda, Rosalind Russell, Amelia Earhart, Babe Didrikson Zaharias. I loved paying my own way and being economically independent. In fact, like the early feminist, Charlotte Perkins, I believed this was the only way to truly become independent. Unlike Perkins, I thought I had escaped the narratives of others, including my mother's and the 1950s, and had succeeded in charting my own idiosyncratic course, *guided by spiritual principles*.

Herein lies the rub – *spiritual principles*: the ambition, competition, and compulsion to be center stage diminish or are lifted. As the mind becomes still and the ego smaller, quieter, the personality can recede, move offstage to the wings, witness rather than perform, watch rather than be watched. Lucy could never do this, even when the series left New York and moved to the quiet suburbs of Connecticut near the end of the run. Lucy and Ethel, now in their Pendleton country clothes, created a new upper middle class stage, replete with suburban decor and chicken farming. But there was only one star – Lucy.

For the rest of her life, as a person and a character, she appeared only as *Lucy*, with her flaming, upswept red hair, arched eyebrows, and false eyelashes framing wide eyes. In her sixties and seventies, her voice became huskier, almost sultry, but everything else was the same. Older now, like Lucy, could I let myself, unlike Lucy, age, with acceptance? Could I give up my metaphorical center stage? Could I take a back row and quieter seat? Could I let someone else write at least part of the show? Like Jonathan, or Dae, or Rob? Could I change? After all, dating, like death, is co-authored. Dating could be harder because the co-author is human, not divine.

The second obstacle: Unlike Lucy, who was rarely alone, I also believed that living alone was the **only** way for me to be not just independent but free -- for me a very high and elusive attainment. Could I adapt to the constant *presence* of someone else? Could I survive all the talk that comes with another person? Their quirks, habits, ailments, needs, and sounds? Would I ever get to sleep? Or find time to meditate or write? What about reading in bed at night? My habits were deeply ingrained after almost thirty man-less (and thirteen child-less) years.[47] I carried on cogent conversations with myself and answered my own questions, truly enjoying my own company. Coupled with my independence, these could be irksome traits indeed for a partner, particularly a forceful personality who was used to being in charge (with a CEO's assistants and secretaries) and who also loved center stage, along with craving praise.

Fortunately, I had learned some things about a relationship from my years of spiritual practices. Love is the highest value and goal. And I loved this wonderful man. I could see the goodness and purity that is Jonathan. I had frequent glimpses of his gentle soul, his fragile sense of himself, deep within his Chairman of the Board traits. I had found a good, kind and funny man. And although he was not a meditator, we were both on a spiritual path. I had much to learn and to gain from him.

In **Buddhism Without Beliefs**, Stephen Batchelor's epigram is from Marcel Proust, and it perfectly captures the life of the Buddha as a model for all of our lives.

"We do not receive wisdom, we must discover it for ourselves, after a journey through the wilderness, which no one else can make for us, which no one can spare us, for our wisdom is the point of view from which we come at last to regard the world."[48]

The rest of this book is about my journey through the wilderness of emotions, a sometimes frightening place that came into view only after being reflected in the mirror of a relationship.

After making the same mistakes, over and over, I became aware that the pain I felt did not come from Jonathan. It came from within me. I could indulge it and act it out, or I could let it just *be* until it passed. It took time for me to realize that my emotions were not inevitable triggers to a response, that I had a choice: to up the ante and inflict more pain, or not, to let my hurt and anger turn into reactions and actions, or not. I love Proust's image of wisdom as our point of view of the world, a point we reach "at last." There is such relief in "at last." But "at last" can take years for some of us. And even then, "at last" doesn't last!

An Afterthought

In Nora Gallagher's **Things Seen and Unseen:** *A Year Lived in Faith,*[49] I identified with her description of a fight with Vincent, her partner:

"It was one of those stupid marital fights in which things escalate so fast you're left with your head spinning, and words come out of your mouth you cannot believe. Worse, I provoked it."

This could be my story: *"I work against myself. I enact and reenact old, painful patterns . . . In the early days of therapy, I thought, Well, now I know about this, I'll change. To my astonishment, it was nearly impossible. I had formed a complete self around unconscious, simple rules: I won't get what I need; I have to solve everyone's problems; it's better to build up resentment, provoke a fight, and then lick my wounds in private."* (136)

Gradually, through therapy, Jungian analysis, she *"found an antidote to poison." "These experiences built up in me, into memory, making a place and a voice inside myself that was less anxious, more forgiving, and had a longer sense of time. But it was . . . painstakingly slow . . . My new behavior got good results, but it necessitated a new identity . . . if the old rules didn't hold, how was I to understand my life?"* (137)

What a perfect question: If the old rules didn't hold, how was I to understand my life?

An Asian Odyssey: *Buddhist Boot Camp*

Centuries ago, Buddhism spread from India throughout Asia, taking two general forms: *Mahayana* and *Theravada*. "*Mahayana* Buddhism shapes the cultures of China, Korea, Japan, Nepal, Tibet, and Vietnam. The most widely known of the *Mahayana* systems is *Zen*, in Japan, Korea, Vietnam, and the U.S. The *Theravada* system of practice prevails . . . in Sri Lanka, Thailand, Burma, Laos and Cambodia."[50] The most significant difference is that "The more popular *Mahayana* school virtually deified . . . the Buddha as an eternal presence in the lives of the people." "*Theravada* stress[ed] the importance of yoga." (Armstrong, **Buddha,** xxiii)

From 2003 to 2006, Jonathan and I traveled to *all* these Asian countries, excepting Sri Lanka, and adding Bhutan. The experience was magical and deeply moving. That our travels paralleled the historical spread of Buddhism is, in retrospect, more than coincidence. But it was not something we consciously planned or even realized at the time. We simply felt that these were the places we needed to explore and *experience.*

Were we simply curious tourists or were we on a pilgrimage? I think a bit of both – the quest for adventure mingled with the quiet sense of history. As I look back, the guidance was so subtle and soft that I failed to notice. But maybe the universe's plan only emerges in retrospect for some of us.

We visited hundreds of Buddhist temples and monasteries -- spinning prayer wheels, pranaming (kneeling and bowing), meditating, and making offerings. The exotic and the sacred merged in these old and holy places. Jonathan engaged countless saffron robed monks living in and tending these sites in conversations. For him, language was never a barrier. In all the countries, the monks ended up smiling, or laughing, as did the children who would inevitably surround him. He always left an offering, along with joy and good will.

In 2003, we traveled with a small group of twelve, led by Geographic Expeditions, through the Himalayas in Tibet, Nepal and Bhutan. When the Chinese cancelled our airline tickets out of Tibet, we made a night time trek in SUVs through the Himalayas, walking across the border to Nepal. In 2004 we spent six weeks in Vietnam, Cambodia, Laos, Myanmar (Burma), and Thailand, initially with a CEO group in Hanoi and Saigon. The journey back through the aftereffects of the Vietnam War, or as the Vietnamese call it, the American War, paralleled the Iraq War (another *American* War), which we watched in our hotel rooms on CNN's international channel in a devastating juxtaposition.

One thing was very clear – Vietnam is on the entrepreneurial move, with more than one-half of the population 25 years or younger. They could soon own all of Southeast Asia. In 2005, we marveled at China's economic and architectural growth, visiting the major cities and its huge dam project, the Three Gorges, an explosion of construction that is a wonder of the 21st Century. As in Vietnam, we spent the first of three weeks with CEO in Shanghai. In several countries, we took long boat trips on famous historical rivers. We briefly visited Korea and Japan, only staying in the major cities.[51]

These sacred places would touch both of us in ways we couldn't imagine or initially detect. We entered a period of emotional boot camp, a Buddhist training ground in awareness of our *emotions,* and of our untrained *reactions* to each other. As educational, delightful, and moving as all these glamorous and eye-opening adventures were, the distances were shorter and less dramatic than our inner journeys – which were revelatory, sometimes painful, often very funny, and always conciliatory and instructive. We began a steep learning curve. Acceptance and surrender are not for sissies; neither are patience, humility, and tolerance, which take the courage of warriors.

While we both had great compassion for the suffering inflicted on these countries by war and despotic rule, we sometimes had little compassion or empathy for each other – we could become encased, or trapped, in our respective dramas of imagined hurt and rejection – imprisoned in our pasts. That we visited famous war prisons in Vietnam and Cambodia is no coincidence.

In Tibet, we were allowed only one small suitcase. But our emotional baggage was heavy with old storylines: Jonathan's history *with women* and mine, *without men*.

Fortunately, we didn't travel alone. Along with our local tourist guidebooks, the first items packed in my suitcase were my spiritual books, my companions and my teachers. After Gurumayi and Baba, the authors include the Buddhist nuns and monks Ayya Khema, Pema Chodron, Stephen Batchelor, Charlotte Jocko Beck, and Thich Nhat Hanh, along with the other Buddhists I will cite.

Pema Chodron, her teacher, Chogyam Trungpa, Stephen Batchelor, Master Sheng-en, Charlotte Jocko Beck, Thich Nhat Hanh, and Daisatz Suzuki belong to the Mahayana tradition. Ayya Khema, Christopher Titmus, and Venerable Henepa Gunaratama to the Theravada.[52] Their words are precious to me, and thus I will continue to quote them at length.[53]

Although I frequently saw Jonathan as my problem, either a fiercesome antagonist or needy, demanding child, I eventually realized that we were co-protagonists. My drama queen solution to any unpleasant eruption was to leave, to run away and live alone (or in a forest or cave or the local airport or nearest seedy motel). He stayed, and talked, and talked.

I had trouble facing the pain and holding my ground. He continued to repeat and rehearse it. I still have trouble hearing anything critical – taken as a paternal rebuke. When criticized, whether justly or unjustly, I feel the shame of abject failure. It is an intense, burning experience, I want to escape my skin, along with the situation and person. The friction, sometimes grating and often painful, is helping me to see myself both differently and accurately.

I still threaten, in emotionally intense moments, to leave. He tells me that my anger is "very scary," that my face contorts into a frightening grimace. When his brows furrow, his eyes narrow into slits, his eyebrows becoming vertical, and his skin becomes dark with frustrated rage, I can see myself. We mirror our anger. It's not a pretty sight for either of us. Particularly for two people who see themselves as happy and kind, loving and tolerant, highly intelligent and modest, and great fun to be with.

Jonathan is such an energetic masculine personality that it took me years to see, and then believe, his extreme fragility. He is easily, inadvertently, wounded and feels things intensely and deeply. I am learning to honor his feelings, to believe in their reality. And to accept responsibility for my triggering actions rather than minimize or excuse them or inform him of their triviality. "They *hurt* him, they are not trivial, Pat," repeats a frustrated Dr. Beebe.

Ayya Khema described our collisions perfectly:

"The defense and attack which happens on a large scale happens constantly with us personally. We're constantly defending our self-image. If somebody does not appreciate or love us enough, or even blame us, that defense turns into an attack. The rationale is that we have to defend this person, 'this country' which is 'me,' in order to protect the inhabitant, 'self.' Because almost every person in the world does that, all nations act accordingly."[54]

I love the clarity of *"defense turns into attack."*

To be grandiose, like the War on Terror (and in Iraq) which continues to parallel the years of our relationship, we turned "defense into attack." Our personal reactions to each other and the political actions leading to the invasion of Iraq overlapped.[55] In Vietnam, we feared the spread of Communism; in Iraq, it was terrorism in the US. Our defense became military invasions.

Initially, neither Jonathan nor I had much awareness of the unintended, inadvertent, effect we could have on each other. Stephen Batchelor perfectly describes what we needed:

"Awareness recognizes emotions but doesn't condone or condemn them . . . Awareness notices without . . . repressing or expressing. It recognizes that just as hatred arises, so will it pass away . . . By identifying with it, we fuel it. The impulsive surge has such an abrupt momentum that by the time we first notice the anger, identification has already occurred . . . The task of awareness is to catch the impulse at its inception, to notice the very first hint of resentment coloring our feelings and perceptions. But such precision requires a focused mind."[56]

"To catch the impulse of anger at its inception" would become my goal and greatest achievement. If and when I could do this, the subsequent storyline of "poor me I do everything for you and you are so mean to me" would not capture me. I would not identify with "poor me," "I" was so much greater than that forlorn tale. And the wave would recede, quietly, and I could see and enjoy our life rather than wallow in the messy interior of my mind. Jonathan was less successful in avoiding the martyr trap, having a long history of seeing himself as the aggrieved party.

One trait would emerge as a central, sometimes upsetting, agent in our relationship – the need to be right. This quality was bone deep. It began with the story about Jonathan's grandfather who couldn't accept that he no longer owned his company, so shot and killed his partner and then himself.

This sense of justice, or of being wronged – perhaps the frustration that comes with "being right," what Dr. Ashok Bedi calls his "grandfather complex" -- would be passed on to Jonathan – who can turn everyday life into a courtroom drama where he plays the judge, prosecutor, and jury. It's always over something that I think is small, insignificant, like who said what first, or did you have a bite or a few crumbs of brownie? I say something careless ("You're *always* angry at me." "*Always? Always?* Am I *always* angry?"), or offhand, or ironically honest, that hurts him, usually remarks that imply a judgment, and the fireworks begin. He feels stupid and attacks me, often by taking my language literally and hurling it back at me. I fight back, defending my feminist self, failing to realize that my insensitivity caused the tornado in the first place, that there is another way to act and react, a way that has compassion rather than veiled criticism at its core.

For a woman who had a thin skin for criticism, I could be critical, often camouflaging my negative take in an intellectual argument, or burying my negative remark in a compliment, a double whammy, and frequently a sarcastic remark, often funny, yes, and cleverly ironic, but still wounding.

Beneath all of the outer drama, particularly my Bette Davis outbursts, were my own deeply buried childish hurt and anger – which I am still coming to recognize. Rather than dealing with it, I just eliminated that part of my life, subsuming it into my indignation about the lower status of women in narrative cinema, there as sexual object or servant, subservient to men who controlled not only the gaze in cinema but the story as well. No man would ever control the Great Me, heaven forbid that he might be offering helpful observations and often help.

I didn't know how to receive, or how to actively listen, only to defend myself or jump to my own conclusions. I liked to cut to the chase, bypassing lengthy explication. Passive acts like listening and receiving help didn't come easily or naturally for me. (Why? I already had all the answers I needed. And what did most men know about women anyway?) Jonathan wanted to care for me. But I feared any strings. My initial refusal was feminism as deprivation

So I knew, early on, that this journey into a relationship would not always be smooth sailing and that I had much to learn. For you see, I hate being wrong and have a killer need to get in the last word. My ego doesn't need to be right, but it just cannot be wrong. Neither can it remain silent in the face of injustice, particularly to me. Why? Being wrong is deeply embarrassing.

It slowly dawned on me that Jonathan's long stories, insistently and yes, sometimes endlessly, repeated, were, in fact, the groundwork for a lasting relationship, that he had endurance --

the ability to see an issue through to its conclusion. Eventually I would learn to listen.

Pema Chodron describes how we use our emotions unwittingly:[57]

"A simple feeling will arise, and instead of simply letting it be there, we panic. We begin to weave our thoughts into a story line, which gives rise to bigger emotions." (69) We fan and inflame them. "So what began as an enormous open space becomes a forest fire, a world war, a tidal wave. We use our emotions . . . we take them and use them to regain our ground . . . We use them to try to make everything secure and predictable . . . We could just sit with the emotional energy and let it pass. There's no particular need to spread blame and self-justification. Instead, we throw kerosene on the emotion so it will feel more real."

She urges us to see the "wildness of emotion," and then befriend and soften them and ourselves, and other people.

Awareness of *"this silly thing"* is the solution.

"By becoming aware of how we do this silly thing again and again because we don't want to dwell in the uncertainty and awkwardness and pain of not knowing, we begin to develop true compassion for ourselves and everyone else" (70)[58]

In **The Places That Scare You**, Chodron advises us to:

"Let go of the story line when emotional distress arises, just abide with the energy beneath the storyline." (28) "Most of us when we're angry scream or act it out. We alternate expressions of rage with feeling ashamed of ourselves and wallowing in guilt.

We become so stuck in repetitive behavior that we become experts at getting all worked up . . . we continue to strengthen our painful emotions . . . but wisdom is inherent in emotions . . . Anger without the fixation is clear-seeing wisdom. Pride without fixation is experienced as equanimity . . . we welcome the living energy of emotions. When our emotions intensify, what we usually feel is fear. This fear is always lurking in our lives. In sitting meditation we practice dropping whatever story we are telling ourselves and leaning into the emotions and the fear. Thus we train in opening the fearful heart to the restlessness of our own energy. We learn to abide with the experience of our emotional distress." (29)

Fear turns into wisdom when we can "welcome the energy of emotions" rather than act out an old story line.

"The practice is always the same: instead of falling prey to a chain reaction of revenge or self-hatred, we gradually learn to catch the emotional reaction and drop the story lines . . . One way of doing this is to breathe it into our heart. By acknowledging the emotion, dropping whatever story we are telling ourselves about it, and feeling the energy of the moment, we cultivate compassion for ourselves . . . Then we can take this a step further . . . and recognize that there are millions who are feeling the way we are . . . the circle of compassion, which is where the magic is." (33)

I can use the energy beneath my self-pity and my fear of being boring and unloved. As Chodron says, *"These juicy emotional spots are where a warrior gains wisdom and compassion."* (34) But for this to happen, I have to be honest with myself, and I have to unearth qualities I have buried, or repressed, dragging them out of the camouflage in old sad stories and into conscious, immediate awareness.

But I could only do this when the pain became extreme and there was no place to hide – and it took a male psychoanalyst and a male partner to create this amount of pain. For it was with men that my problems lay.

"Pain is always a sign that we are holding on to something – usually ourselves. When we feel unhappy, when we feel inadequate, we get stingy; we hold on tight. Generosity is an activity that loosens us up." "The essence of generosity is letting go." (94)

Letting go can be arduous, taking mighty effort. Simply saying, "You're right, I'm wrong" can take great strength.

"The essence of bravery is being without self-deception. . . Seeing ourselves clearly is initially uncomfortable and embarrassing . . . A Warrior begins to take responsibility for the direction of her life. It's as if we are lugging around unnecessary baggage . . . Some things are no longer necessary." (75)

Of all the roles I have dreamt of playing, Warrior is the most thrilling and challenging.

High Drama in the Himalayas:

On the Road in Tibet, Nepal, and Bhutan

We met our group of twelve, and our Indian guide, Rahul, from Geographic Expeditions, in Hong Kong, in the lobby of the Peninsula Hotel. The flight to Tibet was noisy, packed with Chinese travelers. Outside the plane windows, the white peaks of the Himalayas were silent, spacious, unchanged by politics or history. For centuries these sacred heights had attracted meditators and adventurers. Meditators came on pilgrimages to explore their inner world just as mountaineers came on expeditions that challenged the limits of their outer world. I simply couldn't believe I was going to Lhasa, to Tibet! For fifty years or more, this place had existed only in my dreams or at the movies. 1959, the year of the Chinese occupation and the Dalai Lama's exile, was the year I graduated from Madison West High School, in Wisconsin.

Our Chinese-owned hotel was once an upscale Holiday Inn, its glory days long gone. Now the pool was empty, the convention rooms dark, deserted, and the décor, shabby moderne. With one exception in the breakfast room: a bold, wrap-around mural of the Himalayas in the style of 20th Century Soviet Realism. Nothing can diminish or impose itself on the grandeur of these mountains. The hotel was like the city of Lhasa – worn out from the Chinese occupation and overwhelmed by recent modernization.

Outside, however, everything new and old is overshadowed by the dramatic, spectacular *Potala,* the former home of the Dalai Lama,[59] which sits commandingly, impressively, *overwhelmingly* on a hill above the flat city. The *Potala,* completed in 1694, is a huge palace of more than 1,000 rustic rooms of irregular shapes and ornately painted walls that presides over the entire city of

Lhasa. This is where the Dalai Lamas lived and worked. Hundreds of monks used to live in this unique building, comprised of a Red Palace (for spiritual functions) and a White Palace (for political functions).

Now there are around thirty-five monks. The Tibetan visitors wore their traditional, colorful clothing, quietly praying and bowing. Chinese tourists wore western clothes and talked. After a wrong turn in the tour, we had a quick glimpse of the past as the monks were sorting through old Tibetan books, leaflets in a wooden tablet, in a small tower room that was the library or archives. More visible was the present: the Chinese soldiers posted as guards, charging high prices to take photographs, and the energetic Chinese tourists laughing and taking photos.

The magnificent structure is the goal of all Tibetans who make yearly pilgrimages after the harvest, often trekking hundreds of miles from their small farms. Then they walk, clockwise, around the base, carrying and twirling prayer wheels and prostrating themselves on the pavement, hundreds, even thousands, of times. Their pilgrimage can take many days and is physically arduous. We saw old and wizened men and women, in traditional Tibetan woolen clothing, climbing hundreds of steep stairs, devoted to their mission and to this holy place – which contains not a single photograph of the Dalai Lama.

This old, Tibetan architecture contrasted with the monumental style of Chinese architecture. The modernization continues in the new roads, dams, airports, and train routes, along with square, stern high-rises and steel monuments. Tibetan folk culture crashes into Chinese modernity.

The old city of Lhasa is built around the *Jokhang*, the most sacred temple in Tibet. It was built in the 7th century to house an image of the Buddha, a gift from a Chinese bride. (Many temples in Tibet contain images of historical llamas, but none of the Dalai Lama.)   The *Jokhang* consists of many temples, dedicated to various holy figures, and central halls. The building is dark, musty, window-less, with the smell and light of burning yak butter candles. Walls are intricately painted, and peeling, telling stories of the Buddha and showing various lamas. One-hundred monks currently live here, chanting, meditating, and maintaining the rituals of the temple.

Outside, surrounded by hundreds of small merchant stalls hawking their wares, pilgrims pay tribute by circumambulating, walking in clockwise direction, and bowing, full pranaming with each step. At the entrance to the temple is a long corridor of prayer wheels, which can be spun by crawling under them. This action sends the prayers inscribed inside the wheels out into the universe as blessings. Jonathan and I managed to scrunch our bodies into a low crouch and walk the entire length. This would be the first of hundreds of Buddhist monasteries and temples we would visit in the next three years.

Drepung Monastery is outside Lhasa. Previous Dalai Lamas lived and were entombed here. Although crumbling, it is an active monastery, with red-robed monks studying the traditional texts and practicing their energetic style of philosophical debate in the courtyard. Jonathan, of course, wanted to be involved. And the fact that this was a private, scholarly exercise and that we had been allowed to quietly observe didn't daunt him. So he casually and quietly moved into their arena and asked one of the monks to pose the most difficult question to his debating partner – all in gestures, which the young monks sweetly received and finally understood. After some intellectual struggle, the young student got the answer. Everyone clapped, breaking the intense concentration of the debate.

Ganden Monastery is also in the steep hills some miles outside Lhasa. After being largely destroyed during the Cultural Revolution, it was partially rebuilt and is the home of 400 monks. But it was a way station just off the steep dirt path on the way up that I remember: the small cave, around eight by eight feet, of two nuns who had lived there, meditating, for many years. By the time I reached the cave, Jonathan was already inside, sitting cross-legged on the floor, between the two beaming nuns, asking them for meditation tips.

The cave was orderly, with two sleeping pallets, a wood burning stove, and a low wooden table. There were a few books in a nook in the dirt wall and a small garden out front. Sparse would not describe the living conditions. But I felt such joy – as I always did when engaged with the monks in Tibet.

For several years, I had been reading women's spiritual auto/biographies. Two were tales of nuns living in Himalayan caves. **Sorrow Mountain:** *The Journey of a Tibetan Warrior Nun*[60]) is the tale of Ani Pachen, a Tibetan. It describes her survival during the Chinese takeover in 1959, including her years as a female resistance leader, followed by twenty-one years of imprisonment and torture. She vividly describes walking around the *Jokhang Temple* during the protests in 1987 against the Chinese occupation. Along with the monks from Drepung Monastery, Ani marched around the Temple three times chanting "Chinese go home" and praising the Dalai Lama. In the police crackdown, over 1,000 protestors were arrested. (264-265)

Her lifelong inspiration was her desire for the solitude of the spiritual life. As a little girl, she had been a novice monk. When she was released from prison, she went to Lhasa, where she stayed in a cave: "During those months, I existed in a state of abiding calm. No one to make me feel bothered, nothing to fear except the contents of my own mind. Food and drink were brought by those on pilgrimage." But she still had a great deal of fear until her meeting with the Dalai Lama in India: "It was as if a radiant sun had shone through the darkness. All the years I'd suffered had not been in vain. I was finally free." (278)

Cave in the Snow is the story of Diane Perry, who was born in London in 1943, during the bombing.[61] When she read her first Buddhist book, at 18, she knew that this was for her. She began practicing Theravadan Buddhism, the Southern School that existed in Sri Lanka Burma, Thailand, Vietnam and Cambodia (21), but this felt too cold for her. "She then read Nagarjuna, the second-century Buddhist saint and philosopher," and the founder of Mahayana Buddhism, followed primarily in Tibet. (23) But in the 1960s, little was known about Tibetan Buddhism. "Unlike the chaste lines of Zen and the straight dogma of the Theravada, Tibetan Buddhism was seen as too exotic, too odd."(24)

She studied with Choygam Trungpa -- who had just come to England, and would go on to write many books, found meditation centers, and teach and train many disciples, including Pema Chodron. (29) Perry went to India, to a school for nuns, living in uncomfortable conditions. She met the Dalai Lama, early on, along with other Tibetan spiritual leaders. She found her Guru and was ordained a nun within three months. Yet, like Ayya Khema, she felt the discrimination that prevented women from some of the teachings, or being a lama and a core part of the lineage. Women were still viewed as the source of the man's desire and hence as the problem.

In 1976, when she was thirty-three, she began a twelve year meditation in a remote cave, six feet by six feet, in the Himalayas. She ate once a day, at midday, the Buddhist tradition. (86) "She faced unimaginable cold, wild animals, near starvation and avalanches; she grew her own food and slept in a traditional wooden meditation box . . . her goal was to attain enlightenment as a woman." (Back cover) When she came out, she became involved with the issue of women within Buddhism, speaking at the conference in 1993 to the Dalai Lama.

Images from these books play over the faces of the two nuns (and Jonathan) before me. The scene is still fresh, an indelible memory, a touch of the divine.

It reminded me of an experience in Morocco. We were driving through the countryside in our rental car to Casablanca for our flight home. We were late, and racing. A tire burst. We pulled over. It was deeply silent. There was no sound or sight of human life – only a very old man, bent, in the distance plowing his field with his donkey. When Jonathan began to change the tire, the car jack snapped in two. We were stranded, in the middle of nowhere, two hours from Casablanca. We had not seen a house for miles. There was little traffic on the road. Silence, a slight breeze.

Then, from out of this nowhere came a young man – who saw the broken jack and began to gather stones from the surrounding fences, piling them under the rear wheel. He was joined by a sheep herder and his flock of sheep, which circled the car. The young shepherd was carrying a black lamb that had just been born! I felt as if we were in a Fellini movie, or a romance fantasy novel. On our car radio, a chant led by Gurumayi played softly in the background. Then a black limousine stopped. The wealthy owner and his burly driver both got out and began to help with the tire changing. Two young girls in white organdy dresses got out of the back seat, and ran to see the newborn lamb. Within minutes, the tire was replaced, the sheep were herded on their way, the limo drove off, and the young man walked back into the mist that hung over the fields. We were stunned. What had happened? The only common language was that of two strangers in need. Morocco had taken gracious care of us. But back to Tibet.

As if Lhasa were not exotic enough, political intrigue was added to our itinerary. Our airline tickets out of the country to Nepal were cancelled. Chinese dignitaries usurped our seats. At the earliest, it would be three days to a week before we could get out. Our guide decided on a rugged route through the Himalayas – in Range Rovers, leaving in the dark of night. It was a spectacular journey, on a steeply pitched, one lane dirt road through mountain peaks. If I had not been driving the hairpin roads leading into Sea Ranch of Hwy 1, I would have been terrified.

Although the landscape looked barren and brown, every inch was farmed, tilled and terraced; even the highest and smallest plots were hoed, readied for spring planting. There were small villages, yaks, sheep, and miles of brown/grey space, all dominated by the Himalayas. There were no trees, or bushes, for miles. The road followed the course of rivers, running to Nepal, the land becoming greener and the rivers faster as we went. At several peaks, tall prayer flags sent out blessings.

As we came close to the Nepalese border, there were bulky trucks on the road, increasing in number. We left our cars and guides, and walked across a long bridge and through an ominous official military checkpoint. The setting was right out of a 1940s Hollywood thriller -- an international border town, packed with animals and people of all colors and costumes, carrying their possessions and papers. The area was congested with traffic, trucks unloading commercial merchandise. It took two hours or more to pass through; I felt like a secret agent. That night we stayed at a border hotel – a seedy place where the bed coverings gave me the creeps.

The intrigue intensified. During the dark and cold dinner that night, we learned that British tourists had just been kidnapped nearby, by Nepalese rebels, Mao loyalists. Traveling by car to Kathmandu was deemed too dangerous. So early the next morning, at a deserted building site, cheered on by hundreds of excited Nepalese children, we were helicoptered to the Yak and Yeti, a five star hotel, in Kathmandu. The flight was magnificent, revealing green terraced hillsides, using every available inch of Nepalese land.

Again, it was hard to believe that I was in Kathmandu – with its dense throngs and noisy big city life. And then in Bhaktapur, an ancient and preserved city ten miles away. Hindu deities adorned many buildings – as did Buddhist icons adorn others. And the central market, Durbar Square, was bustling with street merchants and beggars. Negotiating with vendors was a game Jonathan loved – and he was wily as well as friendly. To stop the incessant demands by grasping young girls selling cloth bags, Jonathan bargained for twenty bags and then offered to sell them back to the next onslaught of girl hawkers. There was merriment at this tourist turnabout, a cleverly sweet move.

At a local art shop/gallery of traditional paintings, Jonathan spent two leisurely hours angling back and forth for a Buddhist *thanka,* 48"x 48". It is a splendid, intricate piece that greets us every morning in our condominium in Menlo Park. As do wooden book tablets and prayer wheels from Tibet, and calligraphic paintings from Morocco.

The Buddhist mountain kingdom of Bhutan was bucolic, a country preserved in time and served only by Bhutan's airline,

Druk Air, which had two large planes. The flights from Kathmandu have extraordinary views of the most spectacular Himalayan peaks, including Everest. One must either enter or leave Bhutan by air, on one of Bhutan's two jets – a rule of the strictly regulated tourist trade. Situated between India and China, in the Himalayas, Bhutan has a population of only 650,000. 80% of the population is agricultural. "Religion, tradition, and ancestral custom" are the core principles of this pastoral country, its laws and etiquette.

Animals wander on the neat roads, often dirt, lined with deep green grass. *Stupas*, beautiful *chortens* or temples, are everywhere. Monasteries are peopled by hundreds of monks. "There are no beggars, no violent crime, and few thefts."[62] All the architecture is in the colorful traditional style of wood, which resembles Swiss Chalets, with painted, colorful window frames. It's a bit like Disneyland on a grand rural, national scale. The internet and national television came in 1999 and the income tax in 2001.

The national religion is Buddhist. "Bhutan is the only country in the world to have adopted Mahayana Buddhism . . . as its official religion." (92) Everyone wore the national costume: women in long, similarly patterned, hand-woven skirts, blouses, and jackets, and the men in coats that resembled bathrobes, with knee socks. This was the legally mandated garb in this Buddhist kingdom that was largely rural, green, unpolluted by industry or commerce or, so far, tourism, which is carefully regulated. "Tourists are charged a daily rate (then $200. per day) and must visit the country in groups of at least three," orchestrated by only a few tourist organizations. It will increase with the first class hotels and resorts which were being built when we were there.

The entire country was so quiet, so unspoiled, so spare and pure and natural, it was as if it had missed the 20th century completely. Perhaps the 19th, as well, with its industrial, urban density completely absent in Bhutan.

Bhutanese art came from Tibetan art. "It is religious, it is anonymous, and hence, it has no aesthetic function by itself." (75) There is little distinction between art and craft. The makers of both are anonymous. And there is no competitive pricing; demand is known and therefore stable and the labor to make them is limited. Fabrics are hand-woven and paper is handmade.

Despite the national tranquility and serenity, my first night in the hotel in Thimphu in the Paro Valley was very noisy and chaotic. I had a meltdown during dinner with our group. It is still a cringe to remember it. First, a bit of background. Our small group consisted mainly of older couples and two single women. Three travelers were from Arkansas and knew Bill and Hillary Clinton and other protagonists in the long-running Monica Lewinsky investigation. Of course, Jonathan was fascinated, as he always is by trials and prisons. (He would attend the Enron trial in Texas and get to know Ken Lay, Jeff Skilling and other players in this drama, as well as the Scott Peterson murder trial, which was in Redwood City, California, near our condo.)

Dinner was served at a long table, banquet style. Jonathan sat between me and the younger Kathy, a flirtatious, slim, attractive real estate agent, married to an older businessman from Little Rock. Turning his shoulder to me (albeit slightly), he conversed with bubbly, perky Kathy the entire meal, listening with rapt attention to her tales of the Clinton saga in Little Rock. I felt excluded, separate, embarrassed. I became furiously jealous and left the table before dessert, obviously angry. Jonathan followed. And so did a huge argument. The hurt and fear I felt overwhelmed me. I was terrified. Where did such pain come from? The magnitude of my negative emotions erased any tranquility in Bhutan. For hours, I was caught in my suspicious, clanging mind, oblivious to the natural beauty that surrounded me. Even our room, with its magnificent views of a green valley and hazy mountains, seemed dingy, ugly. But it was my jealousy that was ugly, not the spectacular countryside of Bhutan.

Writing about anger, Ayya Khema put it very simply

"Anger arises because one feels hurt. Pain has arisen and the absurd human reaction, the natural instinctive one, is to inflict pain too. Unless we become aware of that, we can't change it." If we reciprocate, rather than eliminate the pain, *"we simply create double pain . . . another absurd human folly."* (65)

Rather than just letting the pain sit and then subside within me, I reciprocated by storming off and then inflicting my verbal anger on Jonathan, blaming him. I created what Khema calls *"double pain, an absurd human folly."*[63]

My upset destroyed our evening, literally, a once in a lifetime experience in Paro, Bhutan, colored by my reaction. For me, this awareness is key. The majority of the pain I experienced came from within me. It wasn't Jonathan's action that caused the intensity of my pain. It was my reaction, my acting out, my reciprocation.

"All problems are created by our own reactions and we have the natural tendency, another of our absurdities, to blame the trigger. We get angry and blame the person, or we blame the event . . . but we forget that we have the tendency inside us waiting to be triggered. It could never happen otherwise." (69)

The "tendency," my fear of rejection, my deep insecurity, was within me. My anger happened because of that, not Kathy or Jonathan.

Khema goes on. *"When one is angry, mindfulness is lost . . . If anyone ever had time to look in a mirror when they were angry, they'd be surprised at the kind of face they would see."* (66) Jonathan would often tell me about the distinct, fierce, cramped expression on my face when I was angry. I had no awareness that even my physical appearance was altered by anger.

Transforming Problems into Happiness, the title of a book by Lama Zola Riposte, says it all. For this is what we, Jonathan and I, have been able to achieve, happiness, most of the time.[64]

"The antidote to anger is patience. Each angry thought must be countered with a patient thought, for the angry thought itself cannot recollect the drawbacks of anger . . . The pain of anger is like burning red-hot coals in your heart. Anger transforms even a beautiful person into something dark, ugly, and terrifying . . . as soon as anger stops, even your appearance suddenly changes." (23)

As with anger,

"As long as you cling to and follow desire, there can be no lasting happiness or peace in your heart . . . Something big is always missing. Your life is always empty. In reality, having the object of your desire and not having it are by nature suffering." (24/25)

Having this relationship would be very painful if I clung to Jonathan, if I feared losing him to another woman.

The solution:

"Transforming miserable conditions into necessary conditions that help us move along the path to enlightenment." (32) "Whenever a problem arises, you can be happy by recognizing it as beneficial. Rejoice each time you meet an obstacle." (34)

Which sounded exactly like Dr. Bedi, who did our "rejoicing" for us. The obstacles I met in this relationship could be a cause for celebration rather than depression? There's a thought. . . But I shouldn't repress them, I should acknowledge them.

In **Anger,** the Vietnamese Buddhist monk, Thich Nhat Hanh, says that:

"Happiness is not an individual matter. If one of you is not happy, it will be impossible for the other person to be happy."[65] We have to let the other "know when you suffer, when you are angry with him or her. You have to express what you feel. You have the right. This is true love. . . . Try your best to say it peacefully. Don't say something to punish or blame . . . This is the language of love . . . When you are happy, share your happiness. When you suffer, tell your beloved one about your suffering . . . Use loving speech. This is the only condition. You must do this as soon as possible. You should not keep your anger, your suffering to yourself for more than twenty-four hours. Otherwise, it becomes too much. It can poison you . . . Twenty-four hours is the deadline." (56/57)

Alas, I would angrily relay my anger, forgetting to use "loving speech," which changes everything.

My acted out anger, my aggressive reaction, intensified by my storyline, has a childish immaturity about it that addressed one of my character defects – impatience.

*"We want things our own way now. When it doesn't happen, an impatient person becomes angry. It's a vicious circle of impatience and anger." One solution is to be patient with ourselves. "If not, we will be impatient with others' deficiencies, we do not appreciate ourselves or others." ((Khema, **Being Nobody Going Nowhere**, 144, 145)*

If I had been patient during the dinner, rather than dramatically racing off, "not appreciating ourselves or others," the interlude would not have exploded into a scene.

On a general level, Ayya Khema analyzed the destructive quality of negative emotions.

"When we get upset, angry, worried, fearful, envious, jealous, and greedy . . . there is no security to be found. We're not reliable . . . and we have no self-confidence. Only when the emotions are brought under control and there is a feeling of security inside oneself that no matter what happens the reaction is going to be mild and equitable, then one feels self-assured." (84)

I love the idea that "security" is to be found within me, a security and self-assurance that has little to do with who or what are around me.

Cultivating patience, along with "loving kindness, compassion, sympathetic joy, and equanimity" are Buddhist solutions for anger and jealousy. And they all feel so good! As Khema says, *"joy with others is a sure antidote for depression."* The result: not just smoother relations with others, but *self-*

confidence, *self*-assurance, all missing in anger, jealousy, envy, greed, and fear.

Gaining control of (or better, befriending and taming) my wild emotions was (and is) no small task for me. I truly believed that if emotions were ignited, it was inevitable that they would play out. If I didn't react strongly to others,' particularly men's, behavior I deemed "disrespectful," then I would be a wimp, a weak woman. I needed to talk back, to speak up, to defend myself. I was on defensive guard, ever alert for a slight. Yes, I was dramatic to hysterical, a Joan Crawford wannabe, but it was not my fault. I was innocent, merely protecting myself in order not to be a victim. I took no responsibility for my reactions. I blamed Jonathan, and then my father, and then social structures.

Not only was I emotionally challenged, but I had a limited concept of love. Although I had learned another, more expansive and generous model in Siddha Yoga, I had not yet put it into practice with a partner. I had changed my mind but not my experience – and there is a big difference between the two. I had the words but not the reality.

Ayya Khema warned about the danger of words: We can believe that because we have read, or said, the words, *"we've actually done it."* But *"one hasn't changed oneself yet."* (73) The words are only a landmark, a street sign. It takes practice to turn them into reality. It took me several years, and then some, of daily effort.

For Khema, if we are *attached* to people:

"That attachment creates hate, not towards the people we are attached to, but towards the idea that they might be lost. There is fear and we can only fear what we hate. Therefore the

purity of love is lost. The attachment makes it impure and thus less satisfying. No total fulfillment can be found." (37)

"Love without attachment is the only kind of love that has no fear in it and is therefore pure. Love with attachment is a fetter. It consists of waves of emotion and usually creates invisible iron bands. Real love is love without clinging, it's giving without expectation, it's standing next to rather than leaning on." (140)

I wanted to stand beside a partner, I wanted to love without fear, what Khema calls "pure love," love "without clinging." To do this, I needed to believe that "everything happens for the best," and that I would be cared for, no matter what would happen in the future. This is what Gurumayi had taught me. And I had learned to do this with my son's medical problems and with my mother's death. But the Buddhist logic appealed to my egocentric nature, and it was, to me, a pragmatic answer.

The best way to discover "pure love" is to focus on *being loving* rather than *being loved*.[66] As Khema revealed:

"Most people are looking for someone to love them. That someone loves us doesn't mean that we are loving. The other person is feeling the love. We don't feel a thing. All we feel is gratification that somebody has found us lovable. That makes the ego bigger. But loving others goes in the direction of making the ego smaller. The more love we can extend, the more people we can include in it, and the more love we have." (41)

Extending what Buddhists call *loving kindness* can not only assuage the negative emotions, including attachment, but it makes the ego smaller. And a big ego is the repository of fear, a place of loneliness, not love.

Southeast Asia: The Silence of History

Vietnam, Cambodia, Myanmar, Laos, & Thailand

In April 2004, close to the Asian New Year, we were in Vietnam, at the beginning of six intense and lovely weeks in five countries in Southeast Asia. Never did I imagine that I would be in Vietnam, yet something feels eerily familiar, as if I were haunted. I remember so many of the cities' names, scenes of famous battles, from the graphically visual nightly TV news in the 1970s. I can hear Walter Cronkite or Chet Huntley saying "Danang" or "Haiphon."

(During this same period now thirty years ago, my disillusionment and restlessness with marriage increased to such a pitch that I got divorced and began the adventure of being a single parent and becoming what was then called a "liberated woman." [Marriage became a "no-never" for me.] "Liberation" was also at stake in the Vietnam War.)

This time, I am seeing the countries caught up in that war with my own eyes, not through media words and images. And I am beginning to feel and to think very differently about marriage and relationships, to say nothing about the meaning of "liberation." This personal view is very different. Rather than an enemy, a violent aggressor, I see a peaceful people, small in stature yet vastly ambitious, savvy in business. Cold War paranoia is what we shared from afar. The fear that drove the war in Vietnam is, in retrospect, incomprehensible. Although it is changing rapidly, Vietnam is still largely rural, a green land of rice paddies, oxen, small villages and farms that we massively bombed and poisoned. The domino theory in Vietnam makes as much (non) sense as the war in Iraq – excuses for military actions in the name of security and protection.

I am realizing that my life has been framed by **four** wars, events that linger and overlap in later decades. As I wrote in an initial and discarded first chapter, "I had just started walking when WW II began in 1941. I have memories of scarcity, of looking up and waiting in long ration lines for eggs and sugar. I remember the preciousness of money, of a fifty-cent coin. Then came my parents' post-war move to the suburbs, and 1950s upward mobility – a domestic consumer surge fueled by Cold War paranoia, nuclear fear, and double standards."

The Cold War inculcated a fear of the dark and the night as I imagined the sound of every plane's engine as "Russians" bombing the US. The second war was in Korea. "I loved (and later wrote about) Lucy in the 1950s and remember (and later wrote about) where I was when Kennedy was shot in the 1960s." My third war was the Vietnam War. "The anti-war and women's liberation movements in the 1970s changed the course of my intellectual and personal life."

"Since 9/11, 2001, my history has been refiguring itself. The Wars in Iraq, my fourth war, and the 2004 presidential election replayed Vietnam; the attack on the World Trade Center, remembering the Kennedy assassination, has unleashed a war on terror driven by fear and paranoia, similar to the Cold War. Like the 1950s, homes have become the focal point of the economy – paradoxically serving as both the equity for, and the repository of, consumer durables. The student youth movement of the late 1960s and 1970s has morphed into an obsession with being and looking young."

Traveling to Southeast Asia intersects with this past – and in many ways, the countries are suspended in this time period. Development was halted forty years ago, and is only beginning to resume again. Recently open to trade and tourism, the communist regimes are still in power, yet changing with prosperity and mini versions of market economies.

Hanoi! I could hardly believe it. I can still see images of Jane Fonda from grainy film clips during her controversial visit to North Vietnam. French colonial architecture and design survived the U.S. bombing. Our hotel, the graceful, lovely Metropole, is a restored French building. (We would repeat this elegant turn of the century experience in Cambodia, in Phnom Penh at the Hotel Le Royal and the Grand Hotel D'Angkor in Siem Reap.) I love Hanoi! which is the heart of a burgeoning art scene, galleries springing up all over the city. Several large oil paintings will journey to Sea Ranch, carefully packed in hand-made wooden crates.[67]

Although bustling, there is a pastoral quality about the city; in the middle is a lake (Hoan Kiem Lake), a place of quiet, peaceful tranquility. Early in the morning hundreds of Vietnamese slowly and gracefully performed Tai Chi in the park. There are few automobiles on the streets. Instead, thousands of bicycles and motorbikes swarm around the city square and streets, in choreographed patterns and lines.

At the Temple of Literature, the first national university, constructed in 1076, the names of great teachers were engraved on stone tablets, along with "laureates" who went on to become famous scholars. The university was dedicated to Confucius, a revered teacher and politician and spiritual leader. I felt connected to this culturally important site that honors scholars and education.

The most astonishing moment was standing in Ho Chi Minh Square (Ba Dinh Square), a vast expanse of open space. With its huge, towering mausoleum, in the monumental Chinese style, it is an experience of power and awe – particularly when compared to the simplicity and silence of Ho Chi Minh's residence. His traditional Vietnamese house was built of wood; it is small, spare, with two stories and porches open to the outdoors. There is little furniture. It is simplicity itself. He chose not to live in the palace of the French Governor which had been built in 1906, preferring a more modest place, built in 1958 on the grounds of what is now the Presidential Palace. Standing in Ho Chi Minh's home, I can feel the air and sun and hear the wind. This tranquility and humility is in contrast to old media images of Hanoi.

Standing in Hoa Lo Prison -- where U.S. soldiers including Senator John McCain and Pete Petersen, formerly U.S. Ambassador to Vietnam and our companion/educator on this trip, were held captive for years -- was an intense experience. We all imagined the scenario in this dark, cramped space, and realized that few of us would have been able to endure.

Hoa Lo was a French prison, built in 1896, and the largest of a network of prisons built to counteract anti-colonialism. During this time, many leaders of the Vietnamese revolutionary movement were imprisoned.

From August 1964 until March 1973, "it was used to detain American pilots whose aircraft had been shot down over Hanoi whilst bombing or attacking the North Vietnamese people. It was during this period that the Americans gave Hoa Lo the nickname 'Hanoi Hilton.'" Only 1/3 of the prison remains, the rest demolished in 1993 for a high rise, modern hotel. What remains is now a memorial "to the revolutionaries incarcerated here who gave their lives for their country." The different occupants portray very different memories, dependent on point of view.

CEO arranged spectacular side trips from Hanoi: to the Mekong River, Ha Long Bay, and China Beach. Ha Long Bay, "with more than 1600 limestone formations, caves and grottoes" is a place of magical fantasy. The fanciful bay is populated by fisher people who live on flat boats that are moored in the deep water, a mobile community that included floating restaurants and stores. Ha Long Bay is two hours from the industrial city of Hai Phong, the setting for an historical drama when the U.S. bombed the harbor. I felt as if I were familiar with Hai Phong, almost as if I had been there. But it looked nothing like I imagined. The city was booming with industry and new construction.

Signs of the war were not only in my memory. Da Nang, a key port in Central Vietnam, still has bomb craters, turned into fishponds, in the middle of their rice paddies. Da Nang was a major U.S. Marine base and the setting for fierce fighting when it fell to "the Communists" in 1975. Today, because it is close to miles of sandy ocean beaches, it is a portal for tourism, development mapped out by new roads, building sites, and a few commercial buildings, empty, waiting for business tenants. The plots have been prepared, awkwardly awaiting the tourist influx. We stayed at the German owned Furama Resort, a luxurious enclave just down the beach from China Beach, the setting for a former U.S. military hospital and television series. The beach is vast, beautiful, almost empty, with only a few tourists.

. Why couldn't I call Saigon by its new name, Ho Chi Minh City? Because Saigon was a name that had permanently etched itself in my brain. As we learned from our many Vietnamese guides, the difference between South and North Vietnam is still operative in personal histories, although the North officially forgave South Vietnamese after the war if they confessed. Saigon is busier, noisier, more commercial than Hanoi. The hotels are glitzier, as are the shopping districts.

The place that houses the war history museum is almost ramshackle, concealed on a side street, with virtually no signage. The American War Museum, or The War Remnants Museum, is a jumble of temporary buildings that tell the war story through photographs and captions. It is a profound documentation. The plastic coatings on the photos are dulled, the edges of the paper frayed, but the statistics of Agent Orange, the brief stories of massacres, and the extraordinary force of the photos reveal a harsh truth – the US was a brutal aggressor.

Outside, among the five small exhibit buildings, parked tour buses are interspersed with massive U.S. tanks, flamethrowers, fighter planes, huge B 52 bombs, and artillery, along with tiger cages for torturing captured Viet Cong. Even on such a hot humid day, the little buildings are packed. But there is little noise. The silence of terrible actions is heavy.

The small brochure begins with a quote by Robert McNamara: "Yet we were wrong, terribly wrong. We owe it to future generations to explain why."[68]   The statistics it marshals are brutal: "543,000 soldiers, 7,850,000 tons of bombs, 75,000,000 liters of defoliants sprayed over the country. Nearly 3 million Vietnamese were killed, and 4 million others injured. Over 58,000 American army men died in the war . . . human beings will not tolerate such a disaster happening again, neither in Vietnam nor anywhere on the planet."   The most brutal photographs starkly show bodies burned black by napalm, or men being thrown from flying helicopters, or a bombed hospital, and color photos of the massacre at "Son My" (My Lai) village. 504 people were killed."[69]

During the war, Thich Nhat Hanh, a Vietnamese Buddhist monk, toured the U.S. for peace [70] Born in Central Vietnam, he entered the Buddhist monastery when he was sixteen, a few miles from Hue. (3)[71] After his ordination in 1949, he moved to Saigon. "A younger generation of Buddhist monks was eager for Buddhism to emerge from its ivory tower and to become engaged with social realities." (4) He had seen the French occupation, the Japanese in WW II, and then in 1954, the division into the communist north and the capitalist south.

In 1962, he accepted a fellowship at Princeton University to teach Buddhist studies. His first book, **A Rose for Your Pocket**, was "an encouragement" to "enjoy the most simple and beautiful things in life." (7) In 1963, he taught at Columbia, and by then "the oppressive measures of the Diem regime in South Vietnam had become intolerable. Buddhists were prohibited from displaying the Buddhist flag . . . Electricity and water to the most important Buddhist temples in Saigon were cut off . . . A prominent Buddhist monk, Master Quang Duc, publicly immolated himself as a silent protest. Thich Nhat Hanh worked hard to make these events in Vietnam known and understood by the American public."

The Diem regime fell and Nhat Hanh returned to Saigon, founding "the Unified Buddhist Church of Vietnam." (7) It had a social and educational mission to improve the villages, and a way of teaching that did not impose itself on traditional practices. It was a philosophy of wisdom plus social action, embodied in a unified Buddhist endeavor/community that went beyond its monastic domains and various origins. Thich Nhat Hanh refused to take sides in the War, yet along with his Buddhist colleagues, many of whom were killed, he lived in danger of assassination. In 1966, he toured the US to appeal for peace, meeting with U.S. Senators who opposed the War, as well as with Secretary of Defense Robert McNamara and Martin Luther King, who would nominate him for the Nobel Peace Prize. (9) After this visit, the

South Vietnamese government refused him permission to return. He became an exile. (10)

In 1969, he created a Buddhist Peace Delegation in Paris, the site of ongoing peace talks between North Vietnam and the US. After the end of the war, in 1975, Nhat Hanh was not welcome in Vietnam. The Unified Buddhist Church was outlawed. Its monks were imprisoned. (11) His life was in danger as he continued to write the history of Vietnamese Buddhism and traveled the world working for refugee relief and aid. In 1982, he established Plum Village, in France, a rural community for refugees of all sorts.

Many of our local guides in Vietnam knew his writings and practiced his teachings. They spoke of him with great reverence, surprised that an American, at an event sponsored by CEO, capitalism par excellence, would be familiar with his work.

Sister Annabel Laity, the author of the "Introduction," describes working with him on a printing project for the Plum Village Newsletter. Fired up and ready to go, she arrived for work and was surprised when he suggested tea. Then a long walk in the countryside. Finally the printing began, on the *slow* speed of the press, which he preferred. Sister Laity concludes: "I was surprised at the end of the day when he told me that we had almost finished." This was a "very important lesson. You feel that you are living in eternity and there are no deadlines. In spite of this *Thay* [Teacher] accomplished a great deal in terms of writing, teaching, gardening, and designing. Whatever he does, he does with zeal and application so that it is more like interesting play than toil." (16)

I studied other writers in the Mahayana tradition, which flourished in variant forms in China, Korea, Japan, Nepal, Tibet and Vietnam. "Bodhidharma was an Indian Buddhist monk who brought Buddhism to China in 475 A.D. -- Buddhism inflected with meditation techniques from Indian yoga. Ch'an Buddhism spread from China and "was called *Zen* in Japan, *Son* in Korea, and *Thien* in Vietnam." (Master Shen-yen, 16)[72]

In the Ch'an or Thien tradition:

"The ultimate truth is sometimes compared to the moon, and the conventional truth to a finger pointing at the moon. Someone seeing the moon points in order to show it to people who haven't seen it yet. If they look at the finger, not the moon, they are not getting it. The finger is not the moon. Words, language, ideas, and concepts are like the finger; they can express only the secondary truth, but they can point to the ultimate truth . . . this is something everyone must experience personally. It can never be described." (21)

This author, Master Sheng-yen, became a monk near Shanghai when he was 13. He fled to Taiwan and later earned a doctorate in Buddhist literature in Tokyo. He founded a Ch'an Meditation Center in New York.

He provided a perfect take on the nature of "problems"-- being of our own making:

"Buddha saw that it was more important to save the mind than the body . . . If our mental problems are illusions and are cured, that is liberation." (38) Buddhism believes that "there are no problems that exist objectively per se. Problems have to exist in your own mind and perception. When there are no problems in your mind, objective problems do not exist . . . that everything is created by our minds is not easy to grasp." (Master Sheng-yen, 38)

The Western belief in a reality, out there, a reality that exists in tandem with our senses, our perception, and a reality that is the cause of our suffering is a far cry from this belief that problems are created by and exist in our own minds.

Unlike psychoanalysis, Buddhism:

"Is not concerned with the causality of a person's delusion and suffering. It is concerned only with their recognition and elimination . . . the power to do that is within the mind of the individual." (42)

We can change our lives by changing our thoughts, our habitual patterns. One simple step concerns eliminating dualities:

"If you don't desire the pleasant, or repulse the unpleasant, your mind will naturally become focused." (69) "To cultivate Ch'an is to transform ourselves, not the environment. Once we are transformed, the environment will also have transformed, and we can positively influence everyone we come in contact with."

It is such a simple truth: transform myself and my world will change.

Stephen Batchelor is a "former monk in both the Zen and Tibetan traditions, associated with a nondenominational Buddhist community in England." Born in Scotland and educated in Buddhist monasteries in India, Switzerland, and Korea, his writings on Buddhism are beautiful and for me, insightful. On distraction:

"Distraction is a state of unawareness." (24) "Distraction is . . . an escape from awe to worry and plans." (32) Most of the time "we are reliving an edited version of the past, planning an

uncertain future, or indulging in being elsewhere . . . Who 'I am'
appears coherent only because of the monologue we keep
repeating, editing, censoring, and embellishing in our heads."
(24)

"So what are we but the story we keep repeating, editing,
censoring, and embellishing in our heads?" (82) "We flee from
the pulse of the present to a fantasy world. . . This craving to be
otherwise, to be elsewhere, permeates the body, feelings,
perceptions, will – consciousness itself. . . Anguish emerges from
craving for life to be other than it is." (25)

I think about my many cravings over the years to be
elsewhere and *otherwise* . . . teaching at a different, or better,
university, living in another state, finding a bigger, better house,
receiving more speaking offers and achieving greater fame, and
earlier, having wealthier parents, a more successful husband, all
cravings for status and money. The cravings I have today are
simpler – chocolate, ice cream, a new pair of jeans, and, oh yes, a
house in Sea Ranch with a better view of the ocean.

But I anticipate that with the exception of chocolate, the
others will soon leave me. For I truly love my life today. And I
am beginning to see the light at the end of my tunnel vision: As
Batchelor points out, within Indian tradition;

"The aim of life is to attain freedom from the anguished cycle of
compulsive rebirth. (It's a curious twist that Westerners find the
idea of rebirth consoling.)" (35)

Once again, I am seeking *liberation* – from the worries and
problems created in my mind.

Batchelor advises us to have friends who are "skilled in the art of learning from every situation." One of these friends is my traveling companion, my partner, Jonathan who has a skill for learning from and adapting to situations.

"We do not seek perfection in these friends but rather heartfelt acceptance of human imperfection." For so many years, I found others, particularly my dates, wanting, imperfect. Rather than acceptance, I felt critical, intolerant. But this is changing to *"heartfelt acceptance of human imperfection,"* which includes myself. **We** are human, after all, therefore imperfect, a perfectly acceptable reality.

Batchelor goes on to elaborate that these friends have been taught by others, *"through a series of friendships that stretches back through history – ultimately to Gautama [Buddha] himself."* (*Dharma Practice*, 51). I think of Gurumayi, the Siddha Yoga Swamis, all the teachers I have met in Siddha Yoga, along with my little meditation community of good friends in Sea Ranch who practice all manner of meditation.

For myself, now, I don't search for *"omniscience but an ironic admission of ignorance."* (50) I no longer care whether I have an answer. On the contrary, I love not knowing, because a whole realm of knowledge awaits me.

"The questioning that emerges from unknowing differs from conventional inquiry in that it has no interest in finding an answer . . . The deeper we penetrate a mystery, the more mysterious it becomes . . . This perplexed questioning is the central path itself . . . Fired with intensity, but free from turbulence and the compulsion for answers, questioning is content just to let things be. There is not even a hidden agenda at work behind the scenes." (98)

My not very hidden agenda used to be egotistic – to demonstrate my brilliance, my superiority, and other's incorrectness. (I am embarrassed to admit that I thought no one else knew this, that I had concealed my false pride and arrogance, as well as other imperfections.) As a paradoxical but predictable result, I always came up short in my own estimation; I had severe bouts of intellectual insecurity and personal inadequacy.

But there is another way to seek knowledge, finding *wisdom* instead of *answers*:

"To dwell in unknowing perplexity before the breath, the rain . . . we are poised in a still vital alertness on the threshold of creation . . . waiting for something to emerge that has never happened in quite that way before and will never happen in quite that way again." (101)

I want to be "*poised in a still vital alertness*" to the rest of my life. I want to be *"fired with intensity, but free from turbulence and the compulsion for answers."* I want to be *"content to just let things be."*

"Such a person values lightness of touch, flexibility and adaptability, a sense of humor and adventure, appreciation of other viewpoints, a celebration of difference." (105)

This is exactly the person I want to be.

For Batchelor, like Thich Nhat Hanh and others, Buddhism must live in the world, not be confined to arcane monastic practices. He finds an aesthetic sensibility in Buddhism's core principles.

"Awareness is also an experience of beauty, beauty in nature and in art." "Great works of art" portray "the pathos of anguish and a vision of its resolution . . . They accept anguish without being overwhelmed by it. They reveal anguish as that which gives beauty its dignity and depth. The four ennobling truths of the Buddha provide . . . a template for aesthetic vision." (105)

"Our life is a story being continuously related to others through every detail of our being." (106) I was beginning to enjoy the story of my life, with *"flexibility and adaptability, a sense of humor and adventure, appreciation of other viewpoints,"* particularly Jonathan's, which was not always complimentary.

On this Asian Odyssey, I felt intense compassion for the suffering these countries had endured; and I felt great admiration for what they were achieving. I think the commitment to Buddhism had much to do with survival and with *"accepting anguish without being overwhelmed by it."* I felt a oneness with each culture, realizing all the time that my five feet and eight inches, my streaked blonde hair, and pale skin made me look "other," foreign. I knew we shared one thing – a reverence for Buddhist culture and practices, and that one thing united us.

We left Saigon and flew to Cambodia, its bloodbath killing fields and Khmer Rouge torture prison, S21, in Phnom Penh, and its monumental Hindu and Buddhist temple ruins in Angkor and Siem Reap. The banality of evil is stifling, terrifying, both overwhelming and incomprehensible. 1.7 million Cambodians were killed by the Khmer Rouge between 1975 and 1979. This immensity is beyond comprehension, on a historical scale that can barely be imagined.

Immensity also describes the magnificence of the temple ruins in Angkor Wat, a temple, and Angkor Thom -- a 9th century city abandoned to the jungle and an earlier war with the Thais, stone fortresses undone by mammoth tree roots, monsoons, and intense heat. All these remnants of God, art, and then of violent history are silent. The places are empty of life except for tourists and quiet with death. War and revolution killed even the jungle animals in Angkor Thom and Angkor Wat.

Outside Phnom Penh, we are the only tourists at the killing fields – the recently excavated gravesite of 20,000 bodies – accessible by a badly pocked dirt road and newly marked by a tall white marble monument filled with skulls in glass cases. A gaggle of young children surrounded Jonathan, hands outstretched for money, which he humorously provided.

In the city, the horror is made personal in the individual photographs of the numbered, tortured prisoners on exhibit in the school turned infamous prison, S21, nondescript except for the barbed wire surrounding it. The jailers kept meticulous records, photographing the prisoners upon arrival and after their tortures. The pick axes used to maim and kill are rusted, ordinary, almost small. But if you close your eyes, the atrocity is palpable.

We read books in an attempt to understand the forced evacuation by the Khmer Rouge of Phnom Penh in 1975. Our guide, Suk Lang, a 45 year old woman who lived it, explained it best to us. After they captured the city from the army, the Khmer Rouge rebels told the citizens that the Americans were going to bomb – as they had invaded and bombed other cities in Cambodia in the 1970s. They promised that everyone could return to their homes in three days.

Thus began the forced march of an entire populace into the rice fields and communes of the country – a three-year nightmare of separation that didn't end when another Communist regime, the Vietnamese, occupied the country from 1979 - 1989. When Suk Lang returned, her family house was gone. Two of her brothers died from starvation and overwork.

Like the major cities of Vietnam, the French colonial style and culture lie beneath the teaming streets of shopkeepers and beggars. But the splendor, the marks of economic exploitation, has faded, decayed. Cambodia is very poor, ragged, darkly sad about the past and quietly wary about the future. You can see something like pain in the eyes of the tour guides who very carefully tell their personal stories, which make up the country's history – the tragedy of war, of liberation gone mad, of freedom not yet gained.

Vietnam, a communist country, has been open for only a decade, Cambodia, a repressive mix of the military and the monarchy, a few years less. Already the tourist attractions, particularly luxury hotels but also the glittering luxury designer stores like Louis Vuitton and Cartier, are refiguring the cities and crowding the landscape. Young men and women are migrating from the rice fields to the cities for work. Mom and Pop entrepreneurs line the available sidewalks, hawking their services, selling local handcrafts and recently available consumer durables. TVs and cell phones are ubiquitous, as are motorbikes, parked four deep or flowing through the streets like a great marathon race.

Although communist countries, these are consumer cultures, noisy, on the move, the current generation making up for lost time. Their history – one of colonialism, war, occupation, deprivation, starvation, poverty, and communism -- is so different from mine. So many in these countries did not make it to my age.

The women's faces are lined with sorrow and deprivation, aging them by twenty years or more.

I am sitting at the Bangkok airport to board a flight to Yangon (Rangoon) -- our jump-off to ten days in Myanmar (formerly Burma). Mandalay and cruises on the Irawaddy and Mekong rivers and other exotic places I have never heard of, even in the movies, are on our six-week itinerary. All I have known of Mandalay is that it is mystical, strange, a romantic setting for a 1940s film noir. Once again, I feel amazement. I never dreamed I would be there, in reality. Burma's (Myanmar's) borders and economy have been closed since the military coup in the 1960s, a ban lasting until the late 1990s. For half a century, socialism held back modernity.

But technology and popular culture are breaking through the military regime's hold. TV antennas sit atop the thatched houses on stilts of the lake people, fishermen who still row their hollowed dugouts with their legs <u>and</u> know English phrases from MTV. Hollywood "action cinema" is so popular in Myanmar via pirated tapes that "Arnold" is a familiar figure. But only the military have cell phones, and the internet is heavily censored. Yahoo is banned, along with Amnesty International sites. I cannot retrieve my email, late in the afternoon, at a local internet cafe in Rangoon, now Yangon.

Myanmar is exotic, and darkly repressive. The military regime controls everything, and everyone; paranoia is operative as residents are fearful of even the slightest anti-government remark. Our guide speaks to us in whispers. He is a medical doctor who dreams of getting out of the country on a student visa, to resettle in Europe. He would love to come to the US, but that is impossible for him. We share typical Burmese dinners with him, eating with our fingers.

Although the country is rich with beautiful stupas and temples, and lovely French colonial architecture, much is in disrepair. On our first day of a walking tour to Rangoon, now Yangon, the closely watched state of repression becomes evident. Although there were barriers blocking access, and signs that prohibited photographs, Jonathan (for whom rules and prohibitions existed only as a challenge) was determined to get a photo of the American Embassy. So he nonchalantly stepped up to the barricades, took out his camera, and snapped.

Immediately, he was surrounded by police, forcibly trying to grab his camera, and pelting him with loud questions and threatening him with waving arms. He remained unbowed! Playing charades by showing his empty camera. Our guide and I caught up to this explosive scene, with our guide explaining that we were ignorant American tourists. It took several minutes to assure the police that we didn't pose a threat. But this was a very sharp warning that Myanmar's current politics are very real indeed. This didn't deter Jonathan in his obsessive desire to drive past the home of Aung San Suu Kyi, the imprisoned freedom fighter. Her home was in a former French colonial enclave of tired, beautiful mansions and lovely foliage. But there were barricades on her street. Our guide feared losing his job, so Jonathan decided not to attempt to walk past them.

The owner of the resort on Inle Lake, a primitive outpost, is also said to be a former freedom fighter, now a radical politician, actively working for the overthrow of the present regime. We met him but didn't discuss his past or his imprisonment. We spent several days in his local resort of thatched roof huts in this remote culture only accessible by boat. As for hundreds of years, life is lived on the water. Crops are planted on the water atop floating weed beds, and tended by boat. In scenes right out of **National Geographic**, boatmen row with their legs and feet while standing up, their hands free to fish or farm.   Homes are on stilts, with the lake beneath providing plumbing.

We boated to local craft factories and temples, knowing that we were at the edge of a delicate balance with the ways of the past and with nature.   How long could a place like this survive now that there were TV antennas on a few thatched roofs?   And tourists as regular customers?   Again, Jonathan's smile and engaging nature were magnets for the female sales force, hawking local trinkets/artifacts in their dug-out canoes.   It wasn't that he was a sucker, he just loved human beings, a passion fueled by his immense curiosity about people's everyday lives.   He was unfailingly kind, respectful, a bit irreverent, and could laugh at his own ignorance, which never seemed to bother him.

We traveled down the Ayewaddy River, on a five day Pandaw River Cruise.   The Irrawaddy Flotilla Company was "established by Scot's merchants in 1905, eventually running over 650 vessels in Burma, mainly paddle boats." This was the river of the teak trade, when the forests were cut over to supply the exotic wood for furniture and decor.   The company was done in when the Japanese invaded in 1942 and "revived in 1995 by a Burma historian, who restored an original Clyde built steamer called the Pandaw." Life along the river was primitive – the villages were comprised of mud huts and a single industry, like making whiskey. There were a few motorbikes and more oxen   River life still dominates Burma and forms the main system of transportation and irrigation.

Even more remarkably, Buddhist activities permeate every aspect of life. Shwedagon Pagoda in Yangon (formerly Rangoon) is a magnificent, spectacular golden domed Buddhist temple, on a hill overlooking the city. Like other famous and sacred Buddhism temples, it is adorned with precious jewels and gold and silver. This temple was the focal point for the post WW II Independence movement and again came to prominence in the 1988 revolution against the Burmese military regime. It was the anchor point for the Buddhist protests of 2007 – until the military crackdown imprisoned hundreds of monks.

North of Mandalay, near the banks of the Ayewaddy River, is a gilded Buddha. As an offering, people paste gold leaf on the Buddha, now thickly crusted in gold. In this country, building a stupa is still one of the most meritorious acts.[73]

The signs of so much Buddhism in the midst of a repressive military regime are a striking contrast, nowhere more astonishing than in Bagan, where there are remnants of 4,000 *stupas*. It's actually hard to describe this wondrous place, for there are temples everywhere, now protected in an enclave, outside the city proper. It is a major tourist attraction and a reminder of the power of spirituality. We stayed in a resort owned and managed by Germans, as was our hotel in Rangon. The signs of the U.S. are minimal, at least for now.

I had received a book of Stupas at a talk by the Dalai Lama in San Francisco, a gift for being a sponsor of his visit. It perfectly described the role of these sacred buildings in Buddhist cultures:

"The *stupa* fuses two functions:" 1) keeping alive the memory of the "great teacher, Gautama Buddha, by providing a focal point for commemorative activities and a container for holy relics;" and 2) "serve[ing] as a bond among members of the Buddhist community who view the structure as a potentially powerful instrument for spiritual transformation." (When the

Buddha died, it is said that eight kings divided up his remains – building *stupas* to house them.)

Pilgrims make offerings of flowers, incense and candles at the base, particularly on the east side, the direction from which the sun rises. Another form of reverent offering is circumambulation; walking along the circumference in a clockwise direction. This is "said to induce a meditative state of mind to better contemplate the Buddha and in some traditions, accumulate religious merit."

The Buddhist scholar and teacher, Robert Thurman, writes that

"Stupas are memorials to the immanent possibility of freedom from suffering for all beings . . . Stupas stand as eloquent testimony to the higher purpose of life, beyond competing and struggling, getting and spending. Consciously or subliminally, they help turn people's minds away from their frustrating obsessions and towards their own higher potential."[74] "An encounter with a stupa is an encounter with myth – or as Carl Jung and Joseph Campbell might have phrased it, an archetypal truth. What may at first seem only to be an artistic and perhaps nostalgic arrangement of brick, stone or wood may eventually come to be seen as an elaborate vessel, transporting the Boddhidharma across three millennia." (8)

We returned to Thailand, to Chiang Mai, 430 miles north of Bangkok. On our first day, we visited every temple in the old city. But by now, we were in overload; we had taken in and experienced all the sacred temples we could hold. It was as if my spiritual energy had been either exhausted or over-indulged. And it was a national holiday in Chiang Mai, an ancient celebration of water and the rainy season.

The contemporary ritual involved throwing water on everyone who walked or rode or ran past. There was a water parade set up on the main streets – a soaking festival replete with fireworks, music, high spirits, and Buddhist monks. After being deluged by buckets of forcefully thrown water, when walking, and then having our car window bombarded with sudden and abrupt bursts of water, we decided to ride bicycles, away from town. Bad idea. Individual houses had big barrels of water in front and pails to pelt all passersby. We got soaked, and it was more dangerous than walking. People and traffic were everywhere, celebrating. My hair was a mess!

This was the excuse we needed. We retreated to the sumptuous oasis of our hotel suite in The Regent Chiang Mai – where we could watch a farmer and water buffalo work the rice fields just below our terrace. The hotel surpassed even the brochure: "A true showplace . . . the majestic resort sits amid 20 acres of tropical gardens, looking out over rice paddies to the mountains beyond." The rooms were luxurious, of deeply polished and gleaming teak, with silk embroidered linens and traditional arts. Our exquisite meals were served in our private gazebo, or *sala.* We abandoned any notion of cultural enlightenment, education, or adventure and enjoyed this private respite.

Being with Jonathan made this, and many other extraordinary experiences, possible. By opening up my heart, and my mind, my life and my *environment* had expanded, exponentially so. I was overwhelmed by gratitude. What a long way I had come – from being afraid of a committed relationship to being deeply grateful!

We emerged on the third day, and drove to the royal summer palace and the most sacred temple in Thailand, on the top of a mountain. By now, my mind could not absorb any more experiences, to say nothing of place names. Both *places* were teeming with tourists, but the throngs couldn't override the magnificence of either site.

But the most moving experience came from the performance at the Elephant Conservation Center. Here, elephants, no longer necessary for labor, perform for tourists to earn their keep, taking their strength and abilities into entertainment rather than logging, hauling, and construction. This project also provides work for the elephants' now out of work owners/handlers who used to make money hauling teak, before the forests were decimated, before Caterpillar replaced the strength of elephants.

I first learned about elephant painting fund raising in Palo Alto, at an opening/charity auction at a local art gallery. I bid on, and won, an elephant painting, a work I love which hangs at Sea Ranch. Here, at the Conservation Center, was the source of that painting. We watched elephants paint, holding a brush in their graceful trunks. And it was lovely. The painting I bought for Dae was beautiful and inexpensive, unlike the pricey auction item I purchased earlier.

I was deeply touched by the elephants' graceful, quiet movements, apparent in their performance of log rolling and lifting; I was impressed by the grace and agility and power of these wondrous creatures. Why is it that elephants always make me cry? This has been true since I was a child visiting the Vilas Park Zoo in Madison, Wisconsin, and standing in awe and melancholy, outside Winkie's cage. My emotions were exactly the same, now more than 55 years later. I realized that elephants have much to do with time. When riding one this day, I was aware it felt like time had slowed down. To encase such gentility in a large, rough covering is, perhaps, the source of elephants' mystery. Finally, I think it is their humility that so inspires and moves me. They could so easily crush us, yet they quietly serve us.

From there we went to Chiang Rai, the Golden Triangle where the borders of Myanmar, Thailand and Laos meet – famous as an escape or attack route during the almost constant wars in this region and infamous for the drug trade, for opium and heroin. We boarded a private river boat, a Pak Ou boat with a staff of three and "open air seating," that would take us to the Luang Say Lodge, on the shore of the Mekong River, the half way point to Luang Prabang, in Laos.

For seven hours of solitude, we observed the forests and river life. Fishing poles lined the bank, discretely so, the only sign of people. The Mekong is a way of life in Laos, a source of food and a social center for settlements. "It is the tenth longest river in the world, and its source is the Tibetan plateau. After the Vietnam War, anti-communist forces escaped across the Mekong to refugee camps in northern Thailand. And during the war, the Mekong provided bases for raids."

Laos has been invaded many times during its history. More recently, the Siamese (Thailand) were the overlords until the French arrived at the end of the 19th century -- gaining sovereignty in 1904. Following the Japanese occupation during WW II, France united Laos into one nation. "Within five years, the new nation endured communist incursions and a civil war which lasted for over 20 years." The rebel Laos, backed by China, established the Peoples Republic of Laos in 1975. "In the 1950s Laos received more American aid per person than any other country. In the 1970s it received more bombs from America than any other country."[75] The country is still recovering from the effects, physical and political, of this large scale disastrous bombing in the 60s and 70s.

Along the way are many large Hmong villages. The Hmong are mountain farmers whose main cash crop was opium, used for heroin production. They are semi-nomadic, clearing the forest area by burning and then abandoning the fields, exhausting the land. Traditional costumes are still worn by Hmong, who live in houses of wood planks and bamboo, with dirt floors. Villages had a single hanging light bulb. I remembered the large Hmong community in Milwaukee; it had severe social problems primarily manifested by street gangs and poverty. Displacement and separation like this is an ordeal I'm not sure I could survive. The much vaunted, sought-after modernity has a dark downside.

We arrive at Luang Say Lodge, on the steep shore of the river backed by thick, dense mountain jungle. Now this is an adventure! "The 16 large pavilions of solid wood all have balconies looking out onto the Mekong River. The buildings, of traditional Laotian architecture, are connected by planked walkways." The food, served by candlelight, is simple, as are the sparse, handmade accommodations. But the setting is very dramatic, right out of another 1940's movie.

The night is black dark, moonless, with a single, hanging electric bulb in our room. An intense thunderstorm blows open the wooden shutters and blows out candles, making the stilts and bamboo walls rattle and sway. The sound track mixes jungle noises with wind. I love this experience! Jonathan, on the other hand, is apprehensive, worried (terrified?) about, of all things, bugs. (Not that the shaky structure will crash down the steep hillside!) So I scramble, ducking the banging shutters, soaked, to rearrange the mosquito netting over him. He is not the outdoor type, although he wouldn't admit this. Then again, neither am I any longer. But tonight I was in a movie, playing my role of fearless heroine with bravado.

Near Luang Prabang, our destination in Laos, set into a high vertical cliff face on the river bank, are the "magnificent cave temples of Tham Ting . . . which contain thousands of Buddha images, 1 or 2 metres high, made of wood and coated with lacquer and gold leaf."[76] Begun in the 15th century, this is the site of a ceremony at the Laotian New Year. Jonathan's knees are too inflamed to climb the many tiny stone steps. I proceed, alone, awed by the reverence for nature, the water, and the Buddha.

Our boat docked at marble stairs along the riverbank, right below the Royal Palace Museum, which houses many 15th century Buddha images. Declared a world heritage site by the UN in 1995, Luang Prabang is a sweet, small city of 16,000. Much of the old town is preserved, with cafes along the riverbank, curvy streets with small craft shops, and 32 old and well-preserved temples. In 1990, there were only 300 tourists. But that is rapidly inflating for this gem of a city, still preserved in time. Luang Prabang "is being recognized for the exotic Asian jewel that it is."[77] We loved this precious city and walked to most of the thirty-two temples, filled with monks of all ages. We rode bicycles around the town and took a motor scooter out to the country. I could have stayed here for weeks.

One morning was memorable. We got up at 4 am. It was pelting sheets of rain, and we had a big box of ramen dried noodles, a gift for the monks, to balance on our motor scooter as we rode into the quiet center of town. Jonathan dropped me off on the main street. I stood awkwardly, balancing the box, until an old woman with a big bowl of sticky rice kindly beckoned me to sit beside her. Soon, more than 200 saffron robed monks walked by –

with their bowls, for alms. I bowed each time I placed a packet of rice noodles in their bowls.

Meanwhile, Jonathan, wanting to get to the heart of the experience and be a more active participant, had driven his motor scooter, *vroom, vroom*, into the temple courtyard, where the monks were gathering for their morning ritual walk through the town. He was jocular, talking, smiling, not noticing the silence of the monks or the quiet of the early morning. However, the monks were not censoring. They saw his generosity and enthusiasm and responded in kind. It was a delightfully loveable scene.

My memory of the kind Laotian grandmother, welcoming me to her side, looking at me with acceptance, is one to keep. At heart, we are the same. The differences were only on the surface. It was a gesture I will equate always with Southeast Asia.

In Bangkok, we checked in at our favorite hotel, the Peninsula Hotel, and hired a cab for a high speed, low pass of major historical sites, including the opulent Grand Palace and the spectacular reclining Buddha at Wat Pho, in the Temple of the Reclining Buddha. This magnificent 150 foot sculpture, covered with gold, fills the entire temple and is surrounded by bells which visitors can ring. This was my first experience with Buddha in recline, a pose I read that he assumed at his death.

Jonathan was lagging behind me, like an absorbed child, striking every one of the bells that lined the walls. Our guide loved his enthusiasm. This was the last Buddhist temple we would visit. It was a big finale, and a sight without any distanced perspective. For the building fits the statue like a snug glove. It is impossible to stand back and comprehend the whole.

We concluded this joyous adventure at an elegant resort on the beaches of southern Thailand, in Krabi, the Rayavadee Premier Resort, accessible only by boat.   As the brochure understated, there were "26 acres of palm trees . . .Circular pavilions built in traditional Thai style have spacious living rooms with curving staircases that lead up to opulent bedrooms and sumptuous baths with huge round bathtubs. There are several pools and five star restaurants" and the amenities go on, and on, until they were swept away by the Tsunami that would hit Thailand.

It was a spectacular beach, surrounded by rock hills on the shores, but the inhabitants of the oasis were white tourists, like us. The luxury made it feel like anyplace. And because there were 26 acres of anyplace, there was no outside, no Thailand, no Asia. It was time to go home.

An Old Girl Learns New Tricks:

China, the Market, and Me/Us

Jonathan and I spent three weeks in China, which began with a CEO University in Shanghai, September 18-23, 2005. Like the Vietnam CEO event, there were terrific speakers during the morning sessions. But their words could not describe or fully explain the economic explosion that is occurring in Shanghai. Learning came from traveling around the city. Seeing was believing. Skyscrapers, built by some of the world's foremost architects, stretch into the horizon. A brand new, modern city of comparable size, across the river, has been built in only ten years.

Every detail is planned and executed by the government. The scope is in multiples of imagination. Just the planting along the freeway from the airport into the city is wondrous. Four to five rows of perfectly placed trees and then more rows of flowers and shrubs extend for miles, with nary a single weed, an unbelievable scale of landscaping, a scale of labor that is incalculable.

Like countries in Southeast Asia, there are remnants of colonial powers, particularly in the Bundt, an international zone reminiscent of the presence of the British, French, and Germans. Tourists flock to this part of town with its lovely restaurants and shops, including designer venues, which the young Chinese prefer to the knockoffs. China feels like money and economic power on the move, billions, not millions, of dollars in energetic motion.

The art market has taken off, although we visited the loft painting studios of several up and comers whose work in 2005 was still affordable. The influence of U.S. pop and collage artists from the 1950s and 1960s on younger artists was apparent. These

117

works would soon be reviewed in *The New York Times* and their prices *immediately* escalate. In their own context, some of the images must be very sacrilegious.

On our own, we flew to Wuhan,[78] boarding a Chinese boat for a Yangtze River Cruise, visiting the spectacular Three Gorges Dam. This half completed project, in Yichang (Hubei province), is a mammoth undertaking to provide hydroelectricity and flood control for the millions of inhabitants along this major river. Entire new cities of millions have been built on higher ground along the banks, modern high rises replacing small village homes; millions of people have been relocated, by government mandate. Urban planning in China can move swiftly and totally, massively, giving a new definition to this last word. We ended the cruise in Chonqing, a huge city with 9 million population and construction cranes everywhere. When the Japanese captured the Nationalist capital in 1938, the government moved here.[79]

We flew south, to Guilin, to see the poetic Li River. Rather than take the large, crowded cruise boats, Jonathan hired a private motorboat to take us from Guilin to Yangzhou. We speed-boated through this ancient, world-renowned landscape. The fantastic peaks along the riverbank were right out of a movie studio's special effects department. Watching rural farm life, fueled by only human and oxen labor, along the riverbank sent me back a century or two in time. Life on the river appeared to be peaceful, humans living in tandem with animals and the land, rather than dominating both. There were no high-rises, no property lines, only washing clothes and feeding animals. Scenes like this are vanishing from the world, and the sadness in this loss can be penetrating. Yet I don't live under this arduous circumstance. So nothing is vanishing for me.

The unimaginable scale of China is not new, as was apparent at the historical monument, Qin's Terra-Cotta Army in Shaanxi, rightfully known as the 8th wonder of the world. This monumental discovery in 1974, near Emperor Qin's mausoleum, opened to the public in 1979, with work and discovery still going on. Pit 3 opened in 1989 and Pit 2 in 1994. The entire mausoleum is enclosed, stretching out like several domed football stadiums.

Qin was the first emperor in Chinese history; he built the Great Wall of China. Obsessed with his fear of death for most of his life, the Emperor looked for the elixir of immortality. When he was seriously ill, ministers were not allowed to even mention the word, "death." in his presence. Despite his efforts, the Qin Dynasty only lasted from 221 to 206 BC.[80]

In a final attempt to outrun death, the Emperor built this huge mausoleum, in the belief that there was life underground. The life he imagined was a warring one, with a full army. Pit 1 has 6,000 warriors and horses. 13,000 are in Pit 2, arrayed in battle formation, including chariots and charioteers; Pit 3 is the command center, with fewer figures, well protected. The warriors were life-sized sculptures, exquisitely made, fired at very high temperatures, and individualized. "No two figures unearthed so far have the same features or expressions." (Catalogue, 78) The figures were painted in great and colorful detail, but a fire in 206 BC damaged the pits, fragmenting the figures, which had to be pieced together after their discovery in 1974. Finding one piece per day is considered a success. The act of reconstruction is a magnificent restoration. Like the landscaping, it is on a scale imaginable only in China.

Paradoxically, the mausoleum -- filled with the ancient energy of an army of thousands of figures, permeated by our imagination of the artisan's labor, and noisy with the throngs of

119

chattering, pushing tourists and the ongoing archeological work --
is in the tranquil, quiet countryside, discovered by farmers
plowing their fields. All the action is underground, buried by the
silence of history and the tranquility of nature that has covered
over the grandiose effort to master it.

We stayed in Xian city, in a huge, sumptuous hotel suite the
Clintons had occupied during a recent visit to China, where they
were superstars. We had no idea why we had been upgraded to
this room, which felt cavernous, like the mausoleum. During our
tour of the suite, Jonathan grimaced with worry that I might ask
"Why us?" jinxing our good fortune, but I didn't. (Old girls **can**
learn new tricks!)

Xian is, I think, a more accurate portrayal of China – the
roads are pockmarked and bumpy, most buildings are 1950s
modernism, now decrepit, cold and ugly, built haphazardly,
wherever. There is debris, no landscaping, and few trees,
destroyed as foliage was during the Cultural Revolution.

The air is dense with pollution, as in all the big cities,
made worse by the escalating number of cars and trucks and
industrial, super-sized factories. It feels like everyone is in a
hurry, trying to become rich! hastening to capitalize on this
moment in Chinese history when enterprise is making millionaires
of individuals working in tandem with the Communist
government. China is for a younger generation's imagination.
Our granddaughters need to learn Mandarin.

Our final stop was Beijing – and more famous sites:
Tiananmen Square, the Forbidden City, and Mao's tomb in
Chairman Mao Zedong Memorial Hall, open to the public since
1977, a year after his death in 1976. It was a national holiday, so
miles of Chinese visitors waited patiently and quietly in line to

walk past this tomb. Somehow Jonathan skipped to the front, taking a sheepish me with him. (This took an accomplished skipper, given the pushback quality of the Chinese citizens.)

Mao's face is visible through glass. "His embalmed body lies in state, wrapped in a Chinese flag inside a crystal coffin that is lowered each night into a subterranean freezer." I just couldn't believe I was seeing the head of Mao Zedong, in this famous square I never imagined experiencing. Famous television images of the stand-off in this square superimposed themselves over reality. Where was the tank? The protesting student? (Much later, Dae and Larry would meet him in New York.) We didn't see any other Caucasians in the thousands of visitors in the Square. On the way out, the hawkers of Mao wares found an avid customer. I enthusiastically bought a dozen Mao key chains, only later realizing that no one I knew would want one.

The critique of Mao and the Cultural Revolution is just beginning in China, although one could see the effects of its destruction everywhere, particularly in the absence of foliage and the decay of the outlying areas. So much had been destroyed. There were no Buddhists left in China, at least that I could see. There are few trees and fewer temples or stupas. While the centers of big cities were changing into postmodern havens of glass, steel, high tech, and green, landscaped areas, the remnants of the past were still visible in decaying sections of town.[81]

I was exhilarated by the monumental quality of China, and I was exhausted by it. How to wrap one's mind around the contradictory economics of China? Its population density? Its massiveness? The fact that I felt completely safe, in Beijing as elsewhere, late at night, alone, and this was not true of New York or Menlo Park? There were no beggars on the streets, as there are in San Francisco.

Although there was so much more to experience, the thick air and the noisy congestion made me long for the solitude and purity of Sea Ranch. I was weary of a material logic of more, as far as the eye and mind can see.

We drove to the Great Wall, out in the tranquil countryside. The long lines of backed-up tourist buses at each entrance, the throngs walking along all parts of the wall, made it feel like the Super Bowl or the Fourth of July more than China. I tried to imagine the heroic endeavor of building the wall, but Chinese tourists kept bumping into my historical reverie. The crowded present erased the solitude and quiet of the past. It was too late to really have an experience of the Great Wall.

China felt frenetic, in a terminal hurry, as if the entire populace had to get somewhere or something now, before it was too late. After about 100 feet, I had enough. We have a photograph of the two of us, on the Great Wall, at least a few feet of it, for just a few minutes. The polluted air of China was becoming enervating. My eyes were weary from looking. I had lost my desire to shop, even for knockoffs. We changed our reservations and left Beijing a day early.

As always, the drive up the California coast, on Highway 1, to Sea Ranch was exhilarating, as if I were there for the first time. By now I knew the curvy road well and drove it like a racecar driver. As I passed the farms along the coast, I realized that it's true. Even the cows are content in California.

Where to next?[82] After a CEO trip to the Middle East was cancelled as being too dangerous, Jonathan and I began to get serious about contentment, about avoiding drama of any sort, about quieting our noisy minds, and learning to accept ourselves, as we are, "warts and all," to use his favored phrase. For two restless souls, afflicted with wanderlust and easily distracted thoughts, this was no small task.

I already had my answer: sitting still, observing my thoughts, in silence. Meditation is a paradoxical endeavor -- It is so simple, yet it is the most difficult thing I have ever done. Seriously.

As Khema tells us:

*"In the beginning, meditation is not delightful at all. It seems bothersome . . . with ingredients of suffering. But when the mind understands what one is doing, namely watching each moment as it arises, it becomes fascinating to get to know one's mind." (**Being Nobody Going Nowhere**, 75)*

Our thoughts are just that, passing, elusive thoughts. We can watch them and not get caught up in them. This is harder than it seems. As the Buddha said,

"The one who conquers a thousand times a thousand armies is as nothing compared to one who conquers him or herself." (77)

The goal of meditation is not a blissed out high, or an escape from reality, or a series of fantastic visual images, although this can be part of the experience.

"Meditation has one object only, namely to prepare the mind to get out of all suffering, to prepare it for liberation. It is a means to this end and not for pleasant experiences. Those do happen, and why not? Let's be grateful for them." (77)

There's that word, *liberation*, again. But rather than escape from someone or something, this liberation comes from within.

In **Be an Island**, Khema writes:

"In the Buddha's words, nothing is more valuable than a controlled and skillfully directed mind."

The greatest support for a tamed mind is *"mindfulness,"* which means being present in each moment. If the mind remains centered, *"it cannot make up stories about desires, or sorrows or injustices."* (23)

As I reflect on these words, I realize, with a smile, that most of my worries and fears were (and some still are) contained in *stories* about "desires, sorrows, and injustices," in one form or another. I had repeated these sad tales so many times, they had become real, they had become my history.

If I could stay *mindfully* focused on the present moment, these *stories* would not automatically rewind and then replay. They could be stories, not my life. They could just be passing thoughts rather than triggers for sad emotions. After all, I was not the star of a Hollywood melodrama.

Khema expands on the negative effects our stories of "desire, sorrow, and injustice" have on our minds and hence our lives. About desire, she writes:

"Notice the dissatisfaction, the pain, the dukkha, that arises in the heart and mind whenever we want something. When we drop the wish, we experience relief . . .the dukkha lies in the desire itself, which creates tension, a feeling of expectation

thinned with worry. . .The desire creates a thought process that is no longer concerned with the here and now, but with the future. A mind preoccupied with the future cannot attend to the present moment.

When we deliberately drop our wishes for things, the release and relief generate a feeling of strength, a feeling of self-confidence ensures. The more we drop our wishes, the more powerful the mind becomes . . . here power means power over ourselves, not others . . . Such potential is like a powerhouse from whom energy can be drawn . . . As soon as the mind has dropped its wishes, we can experience the ease of contentment." (119)

The Pali word for suffering, or pain, is *dukkha*; according to Venerable Henepola Gunaratana, this doesn't mean just the *"agony of the body. It means that deep, subtle sense of unsatisfactoriness which . . . results from the mental treadmill."*[83] The way off the "mental treadmill" of repeated stories of woe and worry is to realize that there is nothing left to want.

Although the habit of having and then fulfilling various desires through eating chocolate or shopping or remodeling or planning trips and parties or writing yet another book can kick in, *at heart I have no more wishes.* What is there left to want? I already had everything (and more) that I needed.

The realization of enough, of no more, changes the very nature of reality and is a soothing, freeing experience of contentment.

"If we can see that there is nothing solid anyway, that everything is moving, even our blood stream, such a moment of seeing frees us from craving and clinging . . . Clinging is always connected with the fear of losing, and craving is always connected

with the fear of not having or not being. Fear and anxiety are the natural states of being in this condition." The Buddha saw that "everybody was suffering on account of craving and clinging." ((Khema, **Be An Island**, 120 & 121)

Khema concludes her wondrous little book with the way to get to liberation, moment by moment:

"Being mindfully aware in and out of meditation is that practice that brings results. It means doing one thing at a time, attentive to mind and body. When listening, just listen. When sitting in meditation, just attend to the meditation subject. When planting a tree, just plant. No frills, no judgments. This habituates the mind to be in each moment. Only in such a way can a path moment occur, here and now. There is no reason why an intelligent, healthy, committed person should not be able to attain it with patience and perseverance." (129)[84]

Earlier, she described some of the benefits of meditation:

*"The more we experience every moment as worthy of our attention, the more energy is generated in the mind. There are no useless moments, every single one is important if we use it skillfully. Then strength of mind arises. **Single moments add up to a life that is lived in the best possible way.**" (25)*

Along with my exercised body, I can strengthen my mind through meditation, through mindfulness – focusing on the present moment as a **practice**, something I can do. This is in accord with the principles of AA which advises us to live in the present moment, not regret the past or anticipate the future.[85]

"Unless the mind becomes extraordinary through meditation, we cannot possibly gain the understanding that the

Buddha expounded, the ordinary mind does not have the depth, lucidity, and expansion necessary for such transcendental wisdom." (103) "Full meditative absorptions are the means to an end, namely insight. If the mind cannot become one-pointed, insight will not arise. The mind will remain contracted, dull, hampered by obstructions . . . meditation removes the limitations, widens our horizons, and deepens our perspective. We can believe in the impossible just as children do and trust in the seed of enlightenment in our hearts." (105)

I suspect this wisdom often comes in the form of joyous laughter that bubbles up from a well-spring within – I can still hear and see the Dalai Lama's sweet smile and soft, rolling laugh. And Gurumayi, unable to continue speaking because her impish laughter keeps floating up as sheer joy, delirious happiness, without limit, infinite. This is self-generated, spontaneous laughter and joy and it is highly contagious. It is the giggling laughter we remember as a child.

I might always have an "ordinary" mind, but I, too, long for the "wisdom" of the "extraordinary mind." This light-hearted feeling that arises after meditation of any sort is a childlike feeling of joy. I have felt it often, momentarily. But then my thoughts of "desire, sorrow, or injustice," puncture it, sometimes congealing into an old story of "poor me."

But I can stop this fiction immediately through the self-effort of focusing on the present moment, of being "mindful," which prevents my stories from gaining momentum and carrying me away with them like an inevitable Tsunami. Sometimes Jonathan will look at me with trepidation, anticipating my flight of irate fancy: "Pat, don't go there, please, you don't have to go there."

I used to feel like indulging whatever story was being fueled by untamed emotions and thoughts. Now I know that his warning is accurate. I no longer enjoy in any way the pain of indulgence. Now I try and listen to *his* old stories and complaints with compassion. Not surprisingly, our clashes have subsided, downgraded to minor skirmishes, gnat bites, or what he is now calling potholes.

Stephen Batchelor provides another reason for the central place of meditation and discipline.

*"Meditative discipline is vital . . . because it leads us beyond the realm of ideas to that of felt-experience. Understanding the philosophy isn't enough. The ideas need to be translated through meditation into the wordless language of feeling in order to loosen those emotional knots that keep us locked in a spasm of self-preoccupation." (***Buddhism Without Beliefs,** 88/89*)[86]*

I have lived so long in the realm of "philosophy" and my own ideas, my intuition and memories, my own "self-preoccupation," that the "emotional knots" were very tight. As a result, I had what Khema calls "emotional accidents." Yet my "emotional knots" are loosening, although it has taken a Guru, a trip to India and many visits to an ashram, two psychoanalysts, countless spiritual books, one grown-up daughter and one son, a lengthy Asian sojourn, a trip to China, countless spiritual books, and a seven-year, 24/7 relationship with Jonathan – a complex man, a man of difficult complexes.

Khema tells us that equanimity is *"The crowning glory of all emotions, even-mindedness. Its far enemy is anxiety and restlessness but its near-enemy is indifference. Even-mindedness is based on the wisdom and the insight that everything changes, on an understanding of total impermanence.   No matter what happens, it will all come to an end. . . There is nothing that is really significant except liberation . . . Everything constantly changes, whether good or bad, 'It's just happening. What is there to gain? Where is there to go? It's just happening.'"*

Gunartarama describes a point that comes in meditation:

"You vividly experience the impermanence of life, the suffering nature of human existence, and the truth of no-self. You experience these things so graphically that you suddenly awake to the utter futility of craving, grasping, and resistance . . . our consciousness is transformed . . . Craving is extinguished and a great burden is lifted. There remains only an effortless flow . . . There remains only peace." (191)

And this is what I have been looking for, all my life. This is what "happily ever after" has come to mean to me.

"Happily Ever After?"

In July of 2005, a few months before China, Jonathan left Sea Ranch for a motorcycle trip with his Milwaukee group of business men, arrayed in his Harley-Davidson leather best. This rough bunch of sixty-year old Midwest CEOs, the "leather butts," begins with an elegant, catered breakfast, rides for a half day, meeting up with an elegant picnic luncheon delivered by the host's private jet, and then rides for two more hours to reach the private Wisconsin lodge and lake of the host, where they are feted with champagne, duck, caviar, and other delicacies throughout the afternoon and into the evening of billiards and brandy, their every need tended to by a large, crisply uniformed staff. This is the new motorcycle chic, a far cry from Marlon Brando in **The Wild One.** The trip was emblematic of Jonathan's former life.

(Yes, I have ridden on the back of his Harleys, on a trip from Oregon down to Sea Ranch, in my new black high-tech motorcycle garb. I also have black leather pants. And I gradually began to enjoy the experience. The Harley noise-level is ferocious, the close-up view is the back of a black helmet, and the wind on the North California coast dries out eyes.)

In tandem with this yearly event in Milwaukee, Jonathan had scheduled several in-person sessions with his psychoanalyst, Dr. Bedi. (For the rest of the year, they had 55 minute telephone sessions from wherever we were – phone analysis.) Jonathan insisted that I be on the phone from California, for a three way call. And this was not unusual. We often did tandem telephone sessions with each of our shrinks.

This particular morning, I sat in our bed at Sea Ranch, looking out over the golf course and the distant Pacific Ocean, feeling very lucky indeed. When Doctor Bedi asked for my input,

I reported that I was concerned that Jonathan was taking on too many projects with/for others. After all, he was trying to find the time to write his book on selling family companies, and he had a great first section and title, "When the Passion is Dying, It's Time to Sell."

When I finished squealing on him, Dr. Bedi asked if Jonathan had anything to add. I expected a rejoinder or a rebuttal. Then, out of the blue, he asked me to marry him. I almost dropped the telephone. This had been on the agenda several years ago, before his father died. But after his Hawaiian proposal, Jonathan had dropped the subject.

I was glad that we didn't have video phones, or facetime, because my hair was ratty, uncombed; I was wearing old pajamas, surrounded by piles of books and newspapers, hardly a glamorous vision for a proposal. But on second thought, this was nothing. Jonathan was in his analyst's office, calling in his proposal, with Dr. Bedi on the phone! He must have been very fearful. There was a very long pause. Not because I had any doubts. I was, for the first time in my life, speechless.

Cut to the chase: I accepted, happily, and we were married six weeks later, on August 27th, 2005, in our home at Sea Ranch, with a brunch at the house and a luncheon for AA friends, and an impromptu evening dinner/dance in a large, unfinished space next to our office in downtown Gualala. We wrote our own vows, and John Ford, our friend from AA who got his minister's license over the internet, married us. There are no party planners in Gualala, so it was a do-it-yourself wedding, a humble, makeshift extravaganza.[87] Every member of our immediate families came.[88] We didn't dance until dawn, but it was late for Sea Ranch, 11 pm. And everyone wore evening clothes, quite a change for this casual place.

Married, at 64! And *in love* for the first time. Why? It was not only the insights that came from our psychoanalysts, although they figured crucially, or the inspiration that came from spiritual teachers and practice, it was witnessing the healthy marriages at Sea Ranch. We were surrounded by older couples who enjoyed and respected each other, with few of the buried tensions and irritations that infected and interrupted the many pretenses of happy marriages I had known previously.

They shared the duties and joys of everyday life, along with the adventures of travel. When the health of one partner failed, the other effortlessly and lovingly picked up the slack. At parties and in life, they were like smooth tag teams. They still laughed at each other's jokes and listened to each other's stories, with interest, not long-suffering tolerance. They cared deeply about each other but were not at all solicitous or gushy. The harshest admonishment was Connie, in exasperation, "Oh, Ned." They turned my negative attitude about marriage around.

But I knew I was taking a big risk. I was an expert on happily living alone. I knew the difference between being alone and being lonely. I was used to making all the decisions, to say nothing about having my own way. In fact, my way or the highway was accurate. And I knew for Jonathan that I was a risk, given my short track record on relationships and my dramatic emotions. And then there was his record of marital fidelity and honesty -- at the low end of any scale. To say nothing of his left-over rage, not pretty at all, which ran on an obsessive, seemingly endless, mental track.

But I also knew that we had admiration and respect for each other at our cores, despite the sometimes volatile surface. I knew that we ran deep, that we wanted to go even deeper. That for us, pretenses and easy ways out would never suffice. We were both too curious. We vowed to be *thoroughly* honest, from the start.

(Early on, we agreed to a truth ritual, a little ceremony that would be unfailingly adhered to by both of us. When truth was in doubt, we would ask the other to say "Right hand up to God, on the pact," while raising our right hand in testimony.)

I was also inspired by Dae's and Rob's recent marriages. In 2003, Rob's heart had begun to improve enough so that he began to think of dating, for the first time in his life. He met Priscilla Fung -- who had come from Hong Kong to study for her Master's in Engineering at Stanford, eventually moving with her Chinese parents to the Bay area and working in the computer industry. Like Rob, Priscilla's history was one of being the best student in class. These two brilliant, attractive, funny, and shy computer engineers wrote long e-mails to each other for months. They were perfectly suited and were married in the Stanford Chapel, in Palo Alto. They have never stopped holding hands or caring for each other.

Being with Jonathan at Rob and Priscilla's traditional Chinese wedding – beginning with a tea ceremony and concluding with a ten course dinner -- was a delightful experience. He galvanized out of town guests,[89] serving as a lovely host and enthusiastic participant. The fact that he didn't speak any Chinese didn't deter him from leading the toasting party in a conga line through the large Chinese restaurant with Mrs. Fong, Rob's new mother-in-law who didn't speak English but had a lovely laugh. Dae stood up for her brother and gave a moving toast to their loving history as brother and sister.

In the video of the couple's history, I saw familiar old photos of Rob and Dae as children, of my parents, and of the five of us, together. In a flash, I saw what my life had been about! In 1990, I had been in India, asking for Gurumayi's care and guidance for Rob's heart. My gratitude to her came in large doses.

Dae's wedding to Larry Peck, a successful portfolio manager from Long Island, in 1999, was a magnificent affair in a mansion on Park Avenue. With Larry, Dae meticulously fashioned every detail of a Jewish wedding to perfection. But the experience wasn't as smooth as Rob's. Two nights before the wedding, on the way home from **The Lion King** on Broadway, Rob slipped and broke his shoulder in several places. We spent the next eight hours in the emergency room.

The scene was uncannily familiar. This painful ritual happened all the time in our lives together. Rob was patient, stoic; Dae was upbeat, emotionally supportive; I was anxious, efficient, pro-active. Dae selflessly dismissed any concerns about her wedding. Miraculously, we all made it to the rehearsal dinner the next evening. With his shoulder in a sling within his tuxedo, Rob danced at the wedding the following day. He had taken lessons in San Francisco, which completely surprised us.[90]

I realized that Dae, as she had been doing since childhood, was supportive of both Rob and me, putting herself (this was her wedding!) on the back burner. She was selfless, completely compassionate, once again.

It was an elegant, joyous, traditional Jewish wedding. But there was no Jonathan to share the emotional side-effects. And it almost didn't happen. Because Dae had not converted to Judaism, Larry's rabbi and others had refused to marry them. They were in a panic about what to do. I flew to New York and called a delightful Rabbi whom I knew from the Ashram in upstate New York.

Now in his 80s, Rabbi Gelberman had been a close friend of Gurumayi's teacher, Baba Muktananda, and had an ongoing relationship with Gurumayi. I told him of our plight. He agreed to the wedding and arranged a meeting with Dae and Larry. They loved him. The ceremony was magical. I could feel the presence of my parents and the blessings of Gurumayi. (Dae had placed gardenias, Gurumayi's favorite flowers, around the elegant venue.) Rob and I walked Dae down the aisle, Rob was her best man. Nancy was my gracious and charming date, dancing till dawn with Patrick, her son.

Another recent experience, in 2006, was particularly wondrous and unexpected: a conference on Buddhism and neuroscience at Stanford University, a gift from Rob and his wife, Priscilla. For ten hours, we sat twenty feet in front of the Dalai Lama, listening to talks by leading scientists and meditation teachers on the intersections between Buddhism's complex theory of the mind and contemporary scientific research on the mind.

The Dalai Lama participated in the dialogue after each talk. Unlike the academics' talks, his words were few, simple. By the end of the day-long event, it was clear that the academics, and everyone in the packed auditorium, were in awe of the Dalai Lama, who graced the scholars with long white scarves as they bowed, humbled by his presence and wisdom. It was also clear that the most advanced intellectual research on the mind and brain was child's play compared to Buddhism's system of the mind and emotions.

One significant aspect of the experience was attending with Rob. Against the odds, he was alive, handsome and healthy, and married. This was not the scenario predicted by doctors in 1987, when his cardiomyopathy was first diagnosed; or when his congenital bone disease, *osteogenesis imperfecta,* was discovered in 1975. Part of the reason was Rob's sweet nature and extraordinary discipline in mind and body. But his thirty years of high academic, professional and personal achievement were in the realm of miracles more than medicine.

Twenty seven years ago in India, I had asked Gurumayi to care for my son's heart. And this is what she has done.[91] And more. For she has given me a spiritual path which is the most fulfilling, joyful endeavor of my life. As my heart becomes softer and more open in my marriage, I look back and realize that I, too, had a serious "heart" ailment. It was closed to true intimacy. I had locked the door to even the possibility of a loving relationship with a man. I had been given a second chance. And this time, I was getting it right.

EPILOGUE: Then & Now

Our quest for contentment, for serenity, became paramount when Jonathan's heart began frantically beating at 200 to 220 in December 2006, racing for five weeks until the electrical paddles shocked and then restored his regular heartbeat. For a split second, he died.

In February, 2007 Jonathan had surgery for two knee replacements. Two years before that, it was two new hips. Cataracts and hernias added to the hospital time, diabetes to the urgency of the present. What used to be crises have become everyday life. And this is our mutual future in old age – of the body giving way and the letting go of the identity that comes from the body, including its achievements and ingrained habits. Andrew Harvey puts it better than I can:

"As long as we remain ourselves – the story, the biography, the vanity, the self-obsession, the addiction to the body . . . death will terrify us, because death is the masterpiece of illusion." (290)[92]

Jonathan and I will face our deaths together and alone, and what could be a more significant or dramatic adventure than this, except, perhaps, getting ready for the journey?

"When we come to the end of life we have to renounce everything . . . we might as well learn something about death before it comes. This is why the death moment is so often a struggle. Many are not ready to renounce everything. Previously they hadn't given this a thought." (**Being Nobody, Going Nowhere**, Ayya Khema, 139)

Although I have looked for freedom all my life, I have never thought that "liberation" was possible for me. In fact, even imagining it was embarrassing. I was just too superficial, too material, too undisciplined for such a lofty aim.

But Khema makes "liberation" accessible, in small increments, by suggesting the following: *"Suppose we are attached to or highly appreciative of a person, a situation, a belonging. Can we let go of clinging to it?"* This is a great practice for a relationship. Ditto the aging body. We see that:

"Everything is fleeting; we let go of our belief in the solidity of things. We thereby let go of our attachment. If we can do that with anything, even for a moment, we have won a moment of liberation . . . a moment of direct knowledge that nothing has any intrinsic value, that it's all a passing show . . . this is an inkling of what the Buddha meant when he spoke about freedom." **(Be An Island,** 117*)*

Letting go "for a moment" is something I can do, lengthening the moments into an "inkling" of freedom.

"When we can see that "all is fleeting, flowing, moving, and changing from one moment to the next, we have a moment of freedom. And so the body, its fleeting nature, and our attachment might wane. Buddha recommended the daily recollection, 'I am of the nature to die'. . .This body cannot remain, no matter how hard we try to keep it . . . We are fighting a losing battle." (118)

With age, the awareness of losing the battle with our bodies becomes apparent. Khema practiced daily that *"everything that is mind and is dear to me must change, even our bodies."* She repeated: *"I cannot escape decay, I cannot escape illness, I cannot escape death."* [93]

The ongoing and coming stage of our mutual life is an inner journey; it is a journey of less, not more. For we are letting go of many things – the identities that came from professional achievement, the adrenaline of ambition, the addiction to work and a busy social life; the definition of what a *productive* day means; the need for distraction and continual entertainment; for me, the craving for shopping, fashion, and other stuff; and most visibly, our bodies. We are trying to lose, finally, the burden of old complexes, old habits, old fears and stories, and the weight of old egos of self-importance and vanity.[94] And we are gaining, at last, the freedom (and adventure) we were both looking for, and so much more.

Along the way, we can share, with our grand-children, what Sogyal Rinpoche calls *"the power of wisdom and compassion."*

"The teachings of all mystical paths of the world make it clear that there is within us an enormous reservoir of power, the power of wisdom and compassion . . . If we learn how to use it, it can transform not only ourselves but the world around us. Has there ever been a time when the clear use of this sacred power was more essential or more urgent?"[95]

In January 2007, Jonathan, and I attended an all-day conference at Stanford University to celebrate the 800th anniversary of the birth of Rumi, the Persian poet and Sufi leader. We sat with Rob in an enthusiastic audience consisting of many Iranians. This day together, spent with Rumi scholars and admirers, was Rob's gift for my 66th birthday. The event concluded with a deeply moving, improvised evening performance. Robert Bly, the poet/philosopher, white haired, tall, still vigorous, and eighty-nine years old, read poems by the Sufi poet, Rumi, accompanied by Iran's most famous violinist, small, wizened, delicately bent, and eighty-six.

The joy of lives well lived came over the audience in waves. Old Age made this possible -- along with the power of a spiritual path that picks us up and carries us to unplanned places even when we don't know it.

Being something, anything, is to fully inhabit, or embody . . . whatever, without hedges, or qualms. It is a state without equivocation. **Being 60** (or 70, or 80) is to embrace all the aches, joys, wrinkles, intelligence and experience that have accrued in six (seven or eight) decades. Being 60 is facing the last part of life with an attitude – of assertion and acceptance, of curiosity and humility, all dosed with humor and joy.

Being 60 is prime time – experience has taught us how to live well, and contemplation is readying us to die peacefully if not nobly   Life and death have begun to harmoniously co-exist. We are finding the last of what we were looking for – and we are letting go of things we no longer need. We know that nothing lasts and everything changes. There is nothing to wait for and nothing to want. We no longer wish ourselves to be "elsewhere or otherwise." Any wealth that is worth having is within us – and we now have the awareness to truly know this.

Our many roles or impersonations are no longer center stage, just so many bit players who make brief appearances. Our identity is much deeper than any role. Being 60 is, for me, the fruition of accomplishments – of being a mother and teacher and seeker. It is also a last chance – to do what remains undone, unfinished. For me, that is being an equal partner – a part that was derailed for me in the 1970s.

Mother, teacher, partner and seeker are all born from love and nourished by compassion and selflessness. As the roles continue to fade in time, the love and compassion will last forever. This is a legacy worth living and dying for. Being 60, what a time! The time I have now.[96]

"*Now*" has taken more than ten years – as I am *now* 76, another "*now*." I have tried to adopt all the principles of my many teachers quoted at length in this book. But am I liberated? Hardly. Am I free? Yes, from many fears and habits. Do I have a ways to go? Indeed I do. How far? How long? Who knows . . . Until my death, at least. Have I found "happiness?" Yes, beyond any dreaming or imagination. Have I known freedom? Often. Describe it. It is indescribable.

The Author

Patricia Mellencamp is a Distinguished Professor Emerita of Film and Media Studies at the University of Wisconsin-Milwaukee and the author of many scholarly essays and seven books on film and television. Her books include **A Fine Romance: Five Ages of Film Feminism** (Temple U. Press: December/January 1995/1996), **High Anxiety: Catastrophe, Scandal, Age, & Comedy** (Indiana U. Press, 1992), **Indiscretions: Avant-Garde Film, Video, & Feminism** (Indiana U. Press, 1990), and **Logics of Television: Essays in Cultural Criticism**, editor/contributor (Indiana University Press, 1990.

Since 2001, she has been living on the coast of Northern California, first at Sea Ranch and since 2008 in Monterey, California and Los Cabos, Mexico, briefly teaching at the University of California-Santa Cruz. Her email is patmellencamp@yahoo.com

ENDNOTES

---

[1] See Haleh Pourafzal and Roger Montgomery, **The Spiritual Wisdom of Hafez**: *Teachings of the Philosopher of Love* (Rochester, Vermont: Inner Traditions, 1998). Hafez was the pen name of Shams-ud-Din Mohammad, who lived in the 14th century, in what is now Southern Iran, in Shiraz. He wrote hundreds of poems, and "he remains Iran's most popular poet to this day," 3.

[2] See Margret Smith, **Rabi'a:** *The Life & Work of Rabi'a and Other Women Mystics in Islam"* (Oxford, England: Oneworld Publications, 1997). "A complete biography of this woman of unique personality did not appear until Dr. Smith, published his account, initially her dissertation." "Rabi'a, like so many of the saints, lived to a ripe old age and must have been nearly ninety when she died." 61. Rabi'a rejected offers of marriage, preferring a celibate life. She practiced extreme austerities, rejecting offers of even the smallest material comfort. One of her devotees reported that at eighty, she had a brick for her pillow, sleeping on a mat of reeds on a dirt floor. "She was a very old woman . . . a worn-out skin almost falling down." She was devoted to a life of prayer and sparseness. 44/45.

[3] See the short section I wrote on Rumi and Shams in **Love, Death & Siddha Yoga: My Mother & My Guru,** *Being 50,* Book II in the Series, Aging and Amateur Knowledge.

[4] As Robert Frager so clearly says in his wonderful introduction, "Communal prayers are visible manifestations of the doctrine that all are equal in the eyes of God, irrespective of class, social, and economic distinctions," **Essential Sufism**, ed. James Fadiman & Robert Frager (Harper San Francisco, 1997), 7/8.

[5] In Morocco? Behind their veils? Later I would see them on a Panama Canal cruise, ballroom dancing with the unctuous on-board male escorts – old, retired men unable to conceal their glee at their desirable status and many choices. And six years later, they would become, to my delighted surprise, Speaker of the House and potential Presidential Nominee.

[6] Several family members, including her husband and son, worked on the show, which she executive produced.

[7] "The One" had an apartment in San Francisco. Bob visited her there and all was well. But within two months, she decided she wanted to be with him all the time, to make their relationship real. So she let go of her apartment and moved her stuff to Milwaukee, into Bob's small apartment. They broke up a few weeks later. Bob did write to me, with apologies. The last time I saw him, he was with Deanna in California. Finally, I wish him well. What a relief forgiveness is.

[8] In **Nothing Special,** Charlotte ("Joko") Beck.

[9] This is equally applicable to national politics, including the Iraq War and the US War on Terror – the nation and its populace fears annihilation (after 9/11), a fear that results in conflict -- wars.

[10] In extraordinary events, like facing the deaths of my parents and the loss of my son, I had looked directly at my fears, learning to acknowledge them and deal with them. However, these were big events, God events. Ordinary daily life was another matter, and that was up to the Great Me.

[11] Charlotte Joko Beck, **Everyday Zen: Love and Work**, ed. Steve Smith (San Francisco: Harper, 1989).

[12] His eagerness for me to have dinner at Windows on the World, the restaurant on the top floor of the World Trade Center, struck me as a little strange. But nine months later, 9/11/2001, I would sadly understand. 2001 was a transformative year historically as well as personally.

[13] I met Angela, a wiry trainer, who had married a Mexican immigrant and had two children. Like so many along the northern coast, she struggled to make a living, shifting from massage to fitness and then on to real estate and whatever. You just knew she wanted more out of life than was coming her way. There was beautiful Jack, her workout partner, a gay flight attendant. Soon came Edie, an award-winning young novelist with her latest book being reviewed around the country. (Her abstract painter husband, Stan, from Brooklyn and comically depressed, thought of San Francisco as a *stetel.)* David was a tall, sweet red-haired local decorator, who worked in San Francisco. By night, he was Amanda, an acerbic and familiar San Francisco drag queen who would go on to host the fundraisers for the Gualala medical clinic, with his partner also in glittery drag. Gordon, the best massage therapist on the coast, fancied himself a hands on healer and on-deck therapist. (I began to wonder who wasn't a massage therapist in Northern California.) I met Mark, whose lower legs and several fingers had recently been amputated after a death-defying bout with an infection he caught in Africa. He was a wealthy real-estate developer from Reno. I loved his spouse, Fianna, who would die from cancer. John Ford, a retired PhD toxicologist who testified in criminal trials, loved to talk about western films. He became a reverend over the internet. The gym would be sold eventually to a gay man from Georgia, who moved to the coast with his young pharmacist boyfriend. What a motley, clever and interesting crew, not so far from the eccentrics of academia.

[14] Bill, a chemist who retired at 49 from Clorox to live in Sea Ranch, worked out twice every day. He was a consummately kind man and community volunteer who drove aging or ailing residents to appointments. Jeannie, his wife, volunteered for Hospice; she walked her black Labrador, worked out, swam, played tennis, did yoga and aerobics, every day! Bill and Jeannie were close friends of my neighbors – two lovely people. The Seals moved to Sea Ranch years ago, after Ned's third heart attack, at 48. They invited me to dinners with their friends and looked after my house when I was gone. They defined what being a good neighbor meant -- the bedrock of the self-sufficient community that is Sea Ranch.

[15]I donate to local charities, but I am a non-volunteer. My ego was already too big for old age. I didn't need any more achievements or accolades. But I did feel the need to help the part of the community that had no time for volunteering – Mexican immigrants, many illegal. My minimum wage is $25./hour; Patricia Agis helps me move furniture and organize the house; Griselda Ortega works with me in the garden; Rutilia Cortez painted my house; Martine Diaz mows the lawn/field, and Ricardo Estrada was the contractor for my new deck. Although this might sound subservient, the trend is clear and promising – from handyman or service jobs to entrepreneur and small business owner. Recently, the ownership of four local restaurants has been sold to Mexican residents, formerly bus boys, cooks, and waiters. We eat there frequently. These new owners still perform labor alongside their employees. But with success, they are also becoming managers. Unfortunately, there is little social mixing across these three groups, but the community lives in harmony and appreciation.

All my life, like my mother and her mother, I had done all my own housework, including painting rooms and planting grass and trees. Housekeeping for them was both an art and a labor and hence had to be tackled alone. Now I have learned to cherish the privilege and luxury of having domestic help. I no longer exhaust myself as my mother did by trying to do everything. But I still work alongside anyone I hire; and yes, I pre-pick up and organize.

[16] When Ned and Connie Seale sold their house and moved, things changed for me – their love, care, and good natures had defined Sea Ranch for me, they were family.

[17] Venerable Henepola Gunaratana, **Mindfulness in Plain English** (Boston: Wisdom Publications, 1991), 2.

[18] Master Sheng-yen, **Subtle Wisdom: Understanding Suffering, Cultivating Compassion Through Ch'an Buddhism** (New York: Doubleday, 1999), x.

[19] Karen Armstrong, **Buddha** (New York: Lipper/Penguin, 2001).

[20] Ayya Khema, **Be An Island: The Buddhist Practice of Inner Peace** (Boston: Wisdom Publications, 1999), Preface, xv.

[21] As Karen Armstrong emphasizes, Buddha (Gotama) "took it for granted that family life was incompatible with the highest forms of spirituality . . . a perception shared . . . by Jesus." (2) He left his wife and son, Rahula. Buddha also had difficulty accepting women as monks, finally relenting but granting them a subordinate status. "The Buddha's quest was masculine in its heroism: the determined casting off of all restraints, the rejection of the domestic world and women, the solitary struggle, and the penetration of new realms are attitudes that have become emblematic of male virtue. It is only in the modern world that this attitude has been challenged. Women have sought their own *liberation,* they too have rejected the old authorities, and set off on their own lonely journey." (56)

[22] Indian texts which reinterpreted the **Vedas.**

[23] Buddha also used the teaching of Patanjali on yoga, which he "adapted to develop his own *dhamma, or dharma."* (48) "Yogis of India had

discovered the unconscious mind and had, to a degree, learned to master it." (Armstrong, 49) "Aspirants" had to "live above the confusion of the emotions," (Armstrong, 44) Yet the sacred, "as close to us as our own selves, proved to be extremely hard to find." (Armstrong, 53)

[24] In **Buddhism Without Beliefs**: *A Contemporary Guide to Awakening* (New York: Riverhead Books 1997), he writes that in his first teaching, in Deer Park shortly after his awakening, Buddha declared "how he has found the central path through avoiding indulgence and mortification. He then describes the four ennobling truths: those of anguish, its origins, its cessation, and the path leading to its cessation. Anguish can be understood, its origins let go of, its cessation realized, and the path, cultivated and this is what he had just done." (4)

[25] Letting go begins with understanding, a "calm, clear acceptance of what is happening." He uses the example of a wave - - if we try to avoid it, it will send us crashing into the beach. "But if we face it head-on and dive right into it, we discover only water."(7/8) He acknowledges that awakening "is indeed close by – and supreme effort is required to realize it." (13) "It is a method to be investigated and tried out." (18)

[26] "The course of the Buddha's life offers a paradigm of human existence." (107) The tale is worth repeating. "It is said that until Siddhartha Gautama [Buddha] was in his late twenties, his father, King Suddhodana, kept him immured within palaces" (Batchelor 21), keeping anything unpleasant away from him. But the Prince became restless. During a carefully planned tour of the beautiful countryside, Siddhartha saw "a person disfigured by disease, another crippled by age, a corpse, and a wandering monk." (Batchelor, 21) He left the palace and for six years studied, meditated, and "subjected himself to punishing ascetic rigors." His body became emaciated. He had tried everything but he still was not enlightened. "Seven days later he had an awakening in which he understood the nature of anguish, let go of its origins, realized its cessation." (Batchelor, 22)

148

[27] We both were world-class players. Or should I say we were equally immature? Inevitably, I would cry, quickly becoming a martyr, which would cause even more irritation, and he would retaliate by ascribing first cause guilt to me. He would escalate into name calling, using words I hated; I would threaten the relationship, which he hated.

[28] For more on Dr. Bedi's synthesis of Eastern philosophy, Jungian thought, and the resultant insights that emerged in this brilliant melding, see **Path to the Soul** (York Beach, Maine: Samuel Weiser, 2000); **Retire Your Family Karma** (Berwick, Maine: Nicolas-Hays, 2003); and **Awakening the Slumbering Goddess,** copyright 2007 by Ashok Bedi, MD.

[29] I found some helpful information in **Jung: A Very Short Introduction** (Oxford University Press, 1994) by Anthony Stevens.

[30] That the source of motivation is sexual and that the unconscious is strictly unique and personal. Jung preferred a concept of "life force" which included sexuality. The central role of the mother as caregiver is also different from Freud's centrality of the father – and truer to my own experience.

[31] Jung believed that beneath the "personal unconscious of repressed wishes and traumatic memories, posited by Freud," there lay a deeper and more significant layer he would call "the collective unconscious," which contained "the entire heritage of mankind." (22) These *archetypes* make up the unconscious – and they are "identical psychic structures common to all." (47) For Jung, like Hinduism, we come into the world with a "blueprint for life." (53) The *Self*, the *Ego*, the *Persona*, and the *Shadow* are different aspects of the individual. The *Self* is our greater, interior being; it seeks "fulfillment in spiritual achievement." (61) The E*go,* the sense of "I and "Me," is the center of consciousness. (62) The P*ersona* is our mask, a façade, which we fashion "to be acceptable to others," "a shop window where we display our best wares." (63) And our

S*hadow* is a lower, disowned personality, like the stories of *Jekyll and Hyde*, or the *Portrait of Dorian Gray*. We keep the worst part of ourselves under wraps, not fearing castration by the father (Freudian) but rather being abandoned by the mother for not being acceptable. (66) This centrality of the mother was more in accord with my experience; fear of losing her love accompanied me throughout my life like a censor.

The most painful part of analysis is confronting the s*hadow* -- which is not surprising because the s*hadow* is "tinged with feelings of guilt and unworthiness and with fears of rejection should its true nature be discovered or exposed." This is precisely the way most addicts feel when they begin sobriety – unworthy, guilty, fearing rejection but meeting acceptance in AA. They begin to confront their s*hadow*, where "so much potential and energy is locked away," hidden within the addiction. (76) Or the addiction is the literal embodiment of the s*hadow*. After the initial painful struggle, there is a "feeling of being more creative, more whole . . . to own one's *shadow* is to become responsible for it . . . ethical choices become possible." (67)

³² Dr. John Beebe is an international figure in the psychoanalytic community, an intellectual who was the editor/founder of the professional Jungian journal for many years. He is a noted scholar of, among other things, Jungian readings of films, along with his particular expertise in typologies. He did have semi-trances during some of our sessions, periods when he would appear to doze off. Sometimes I was uncertain whether he was exhausted or intuiting something from my words. I was a very slow pupil, finding it difficult to comprehend things that I had repressed or buried for so long. It took months before I had any real awareness of what his words were referring to.

³³ There are four basic types of perception and response: "Sensation (sense perception) tells us that something exists; thinking tells you what it is; feeling tells you whether it is agreeable or not; and intuition tells you when it comes and where it is going." (In **Man and His Symbols**,

61) (86.) Thinking is paired with feeling (which should not be confused with emotion or affect; it is judgment, evaluation) and sensation with intuition. One of the four will be our superior function and the other of the pair our inferior function. Each of the four types is further distinguished by being either <u>extroverted</u> or <u>introverted</u>. Introverts place great "importance on inner subjective realities and extraverts on objective events." (86) Very briefly, the four types: intuition and sensation, thinking and feeling, doubled by being either introverted or extroverted, making a total of eight psychological types.

[34] And slowly, I am acknowledging the role certain of my actions play in upsetting him -- like interrupting him when he is on the telephone, or asking for his help without relinquishing the task myself. To me, these are small annoyances; to him they are felonies. But the reality is that they hurt him, they upset him, so I need to have empathy with his feelings, which are real. To see them as insignificant is actually insulting to him. This has come only very recently. It has involved what Dr. Beebe calls "an ethics of caring versus an ethics of justice." Being right, along with adjudicating the severity of another's feelings, are habits I am changing. I no longer value them as I used to

[35] Chogyam Trungpa, **Great Eastern Sun: the Wisdom of Shambhala**, ed. Carolyn Rose Gimian (Boston & London: Shambhala, 2001).

36 Ayya Khema, **Be an Island: The Buddhist Practice of Inner Peace** (Boston, MA: Wisdom Publications, 1999).

[37] Pema Chodron, **When Things Fall Apart:** *Heart Advice for Difficult Times* (Boston & London: Shambala, 2000); **The Wisdom of No Escape:** *And the Path if Loving Kindness* (Boston & London: Shambhala, 1991); **The Places That Scare You**: *A Guide to Fearlessness in Difficult Times* (Boston & London: Shambhala, 2001).

[38] Robert Thurman, **Essential Tibetan Buddhism** (New Jersey: Castle Books, 1995).

[39] Buddha "emphatically disclaimed the possession of the Godlike power of creatorhood . . . but he was not an atheist. He believed he had met a number of enlightened beings." (10)

[40] Like Gurumayi, Buddha again and again told his followers not to take "anything on trust." (Armstrong 47) He urged them to test everything. Thus, Buddhism has no "theories about the creation of the universe or the existence of a Supreme Being. These matters might be interesting but they could not give a disciple enlightenment." (Armstrong 102)

[41] We became patrons of the Telluride Film Festival, watching wonderful films at the magnificent event every Labor Day weekend. I taught a film history course at UC-Santa Cruz, a beautiful commute from our condominium in Menlo Park. It was on the war against terror, with Iraq just beginning to gear up in the spring of 2003. But that was it for professional engagements and the movies. I had retired, with one book to finish.

[42] "I found the revelation that I could look back upon my sixties with pleasure astonishing." (7) I quite agree with Carolyn Heilbrun, another professor, who did not find "the joy in my grandchildren, great as it is, half so profound as the pleasure I take in my adult children. To perceive the enchantment of small children does not require the eyes of the old. To taste with special relish the conversation of one's grown-up children does . . . Perhaps because I am not a natural lover of children, the most potent reward for parenthood I have known has been delight in my fully grown progeny. They are friends with an extra dimension of affection." I am thrilled listening to Rob and Dae talk about their work, or politics, or their lives in general. How did they become such remarkable adults? So intelligent, so perceptive, so creative? See Carolyn Heilbrun, **The Last Gift of Time: Life Beyond Sixty** (New York: Dial Press, 1997). See also **Writing a Woman's Life** (New York: Ballantine, 1988).

[43] Jonathan and I also had therapy, alone and together. Why? Because along with the intense love came arguments. And Jonathan was, by

nature, hypercritical. And, by nature, I was not at all a perfectionist, along with being unaware of others around me. (I love to become lost in my thoughts.) We had skirmishes, squabbles, and full-scale battles. If they occurred on the way to a dinner party, we would turn around sometimes three or four times, drive back home, decide to go, turn around, etcetera, before arriving in some dizzy state of frazzled detente. Then we would experience a usually delightful dinner party. The ride home was always touch-and-go, the slightest tinder could ignite into a forest fire. Several times I almost walked off airplanes (to Honolulu), or refused to get on board (in Japan). High childish drama indeed. Why? The simplest reason is that I had lived alone for so many years and had no skills for long-term intimacy and interaction. And although Jonathan had been married for 35 years to the same woman, he had serious unsolved issues around women, and had escaped from confronting them in his own deceptive way.

[44] Ayya Khema, **Being Nobody Going Nowhere** (Boston: Wisdom Publications, 1987).

[45] See Ayya Khema, **I Give You My Life:** *The Autobiography of a Western Buddhist Nun* (Boston & London: Shambhala, 2000).

[46] In Ayya Khema's **Be An Island**, "Forward," Sandy Boucher, 1998, ix – xiv. She spoke without notes, in a simple, accessible style. Like so many other spiritual teachers, including Baba Muktananda and Gurumayi, Khema preferred the peace of monastic life; yet she was willing to travel around the world to share her insights. In 1988, she received ordination in the Chinese Buddhist tradition, in Los Angeles. As one of her followers wrote: "Nothing could be more essentially Buddhist than spiritual equality, regardless of gender." (xiii)

[47] I decided early on that rather than being irritated by his quirks and habits – including a unique piercing nasal trumpeting to clear his ears -- I would accept them all (OK, with three exceptions) as part of the package. I had realized years ago that my intolerance of others' personal

traits made **me** anxious and unhappy and did not change anything. Jonathan tried to accept me in the same way, what he would "romantically" refer to as "taking the "rocks with the farm." I tried to see the rocks and the farm as the same. Charlotte Beck would see the sharp rocks as jewels. This became our mutual goal.

[48] Stephen Batchelor, **Buddhism Without Beliefs,** *A Contemporary Guide to Awakening* (New York: Riverhead Books, 1997).

[49] Nora Gallagher, **Things Seen and Unseen: A Year Lived in Faith** (New York: Vintage, 1998).

[50] Venerable Guntarama, **Mindfulness in Plain English** (Boston: Wisdom Publications, 1992 (Taiwan, 1991), 4.

[51] In 2006, the Middle East beckoned. The outbreak of fighting between Israel and Lebanon in July 2006 forced cancellation.

[52] Early Buddhist texts were written one hundred years after the Buddha's death, in Pali, a dialect of Northern India, after being orally transmitted for many years. These are the source for much of the barely recorded history of the Buddha's life. Theravada Buddhists preserved these early texts. The Sanskrit texts were Chinese or Tibetan. The Sanskrit "karma, dharma, and Nirvana," become "kamma, dhamma, and Nibbana" in Pali. xxix in Karen Armstrong's **Buddha** (New York: Penguin Books, 2001). This little book is a concise, accessible account of the Buddha's life. "What is historical is the fact of the legend." As it spread through cultures, the dharma maintained its integrity and "responded to the needs of the new situation . . . it had to imagine itself in original and unexpected ways (compare the Pali discourses, a collection of Zen koans, and the **Tibetan Book of the Dead**), " 107. They were imaginative, they were not orthodoxies. Buddhism is "the freedom from anguish and the freedom to respond creatively to the anguish of the world." 109.

154

[53] There were other books, the beautifully written **Verses from the Center:** *A Buddhist Vision of the Sublime* by Stephen Batchelor; **Taming the Monkey Mind** by Thubten Chodron, a Buddhist nun; and many books on Zen Buddhism, including three collections of the writings of the well-known Buddhist scholar, D.T. Suzuki: **Introduction to Zen Buddhism**, with an introduction by Carl Jung, published by Grove Press in 1964; **Zen Buddhism: Selected Writings of D.T. Suzuki**, originally published in 1956 and reissued in 1996; and **The Awakening of Zen**, Shambala Press in 1980.

[54] Ayya Khema, **Being Nobody Going Nowhere**, 47.

[55] Through meditation, we will have fewer grandiose ideas about "one's person."

[56] Stephen Batchelor, **Buddhism Without Beliefs**, 60.

[57] And because the words of these writers are so perfect, so true, I directly quote rather than summarize passages; that way, anyone can forge his or her own interpretation; thus, I see these long quotes as gifts.

[58] Pema Chodron, **When Things Fall Apart:** *Heart Advice for Difficult Times* (Boston & London: Shambhala, 2000).

[59] *Lama* is a translation of the Sanskrit word, *guru*, and means spiritual teacher.

[60] Co-written with Adelaide Donnelley (New York: Kodansha International, 2000).

[61] Vicki MacKenzie, **Cave in the Snow:** *Tenzim Palmo's Quest for Enlightenment* (Great Britain: Bloomsbury, 1998). As a young woman, she had two sides: "On the one side, I was fun loving and frivolous; and

on the other I was serious and 'spiritual.' These two sides were at war."
(27) I so identified with this double aspect.

[62] Francoise Pommaret, **Bhutan: Himalayan Mountain Kingdom**, trans. Elisabeth Booz & Howard Solverson (Hong Kong: Airphoto International, 1998). This was the first guide written about this country in 1990.

[63] In **Being Nobody, Going Nowhere**.

[64] Lama Zopa Rinpoche, **Transforming Problems into Happiness** (Boston: Wisdom Publications, 2001).

[65] Thich Nhat Hanh, **Anger** (New York: Riverhead Books, 2001).

[66] "Love cannot be encased in a person. A person is nothing but a bag of bones . . . How can love be embedded in that? Yet that is what the famous tragedies are all about. (38) Love is embedded in a feeling. (39) Love is more importantly cultivated when we confront someone who is totally lovable."

[67] Vietnam was my first CEO trip, a unique travel experience. CEO is the outgrowth of YPO, Young Presidents' Organization, to which Jonathan belonged. This international group consists of individuals who became presidents of companies before they were forty. (At age fifty, 10% of these members are invited to join CEO.) The selection criteria for both versions are stringent, involving a nomination and election process. CEO, like YPO, sponsors numerous events, including international travel, for members and their families. This is ultimately luxurious, over-the-top travel, involving not only five star hotels and services, but first class education about the places visited. Speakers at YPO events include the leadership of countries, along with leading intellectuals on the area. Mornings are spent in class; afternoons on special tours, privileged inside glimpses into cultures, and evenings at black-tie dinners, dances, and

other extravaganzas. The settings for these events will be presidential palaces, national museums, famous restaurants.

[68] **In Retrospect: The Tragedy and Lessons of Vietnam** (New York: Times Books, 1995), Preface, XVI.

[69] When the point of view changes, so does history. Jonathan visited the Cu-Chi tunnels, outside Ho Chi Minh City. It had originally been built during the resistance war against French colonialists, from 1945 to 1954. From 1961 to 1965, it shielded soldiers "operating in the enemy's rear zone," the U.S. As the war escalated, the tunnels expanded into the north. "The tunnels were not dug deep, but still were resistant to canon shells and to the heavy weight of tanks and armored cars . . . there were block-points at sensitive spots to obstruct the way of the enemy or to stop the toxic chemicals sprayed by them . . . there were sections structured from two to three stories . . . there were also narrow sections that only light and thin persons could worm their way through . . . carefully-designed shafts for fresh air connected to the surface face by multiple secret openings . Pitfalls, nail and spike traps were set at critical points of the system. Around tunnel entrances and exits were also laid nail and spike traps, land mines, as well as antitank high explosive mines . . . Inter-related to the system were broad trenches for rest after combat where hammocks could be hung up. There were reserves of weapons food, water, facilities for surgery, living quarters for wounded and convalescing combatants, shelters for women, old people and children . . . and theaters for film shows and productions. All this underground world was elaborately concealed overhead." From the tourist pamphlet of the site.

[70] **Thich Nhat Hanh**: *Essential Writings*, "Introduction, 'If You Want Peace, You Can Have Peace,'" by Sister Annabel Laity (Mar knoll, New York: Orbis Books, 2001), 1. Other books which have accompanied me include **Peace is Every Step**: *The Path of Mindfulness in Everyday Life*, with a foreword by the Dalai Lama (New York: Bantam, 1992); **The Miracle of Mindfulness**: *An Introduction to the Practice of Meditation,*

trans. Mobi Ho (Boston: Beacon Press, 1975/1987); **Anger:** *Wisdom for Cooling the Flames* (New York: Riverhead Books, 2001) and **No Death, No Fear** (Riverhead Books: New York, 2002).

[71] As a novice, he learned to be present in everything he did. "While closing the door you learn to be truly present while closing the door. While cooking you are truly present in the cooking." (4)

[72] Master Sheng-yen, **Subtle Wisdom** *Understanding Suffering, Cultivating Compassion Through Ch'an Buddhism* (New York: Doubleday, 1999).

[73] In **Buddhist Stupas in Asia: the Shape of Perfection,** Photography, Bill Wassman, Text, Joe Cummings, Foreword, Robert AF Thurman (Oakland, CA: Lonely Planet Publications, 2001).

[74] Foreword, 5.

[75] Guidebook, 24/25

[76] Guidebook, 22/23.

[77] Guide book, 26/27.

[78] Wuhan was the site of Mao's Villa.

[79] Our driver and guide, who was a medical doctor, as was our guide in Myanmar, took us to see an historical theater in the center of town. This ruse was one of many tourists sites for "original" art, actually copies of paintings sold throughout China. Yes, we bought three "signed" pieces from fast-negotiating sellers who had taken them down and wrapped them up before we could examine them. Chinese merchants can be relentless and blithely deceitful in making the sale.

[80] **Awakened: Qin's Terra-Cotta** Army, Shaanxi Travel & Tourism Press, October 2001, 10, 11. This is the catalogue for the monument.

[81] We stayed at the Peninsula Palace, which was just off the square, downtown, a great hotel. And we trekked through the famous knock-off malls, where Jonathan loaded up on Ralph Lauren shirts and Mont Blanc pens (100 for $50.00, after two days of hard bargaining), and I found cashmere and silk items for gifts. These warehouses must be the sources for New York city street vendors. The low prices speak of cheap labor and lots of it, primarily by women, in country villages or huge factories. And what if China ever raised their prices? We would be captive. The U.S. has given up most sources of production. What would happen to China if the US stopped shopping?

[82] An eagerly anticipated CEO trip to the Middle East, in 2006, would be cancelled due to the U.S. War in Iraq. We were scheduled to visit Jordan, Syria, Israel, Egypt, and Turkey. We would take our granddaughters on two Disney Cruises, in January of 2006 and 2007, to our mutual delight. We would visit Jonathan's 88 year old mother in Hawaii several times, including an early 90th birthday party, and spend time with his brother, Dave, and Kathleen – a lovely couple I have grown to love thoroughly. They will join us in Telluride, Colorado for the film festival again in September. Nancy will come and visit for the holidays, staying in the Stanford Park Hotel, right behind our condominium in Menlo Park. We will spend time in Boca Raton, Florida, with Jim and Deanna Rosemurghy, Jonathan's cousin, who is like a brother to Jonathan, and celebrate the weddings of two of their three children, in a year. There are regular trips to New York, where we will eventually buy a condo in The Caledonia, in Chelsea, on the newly planned High Line, only three blocks away from Dae, Larry, and Remi; and visits to first Tulsa, Oklahoma and then Portland, Oregon, to enjoy Amy, Jonathan's daughter, Brian, her husband, and our two grandchildren, Alessandra and Siena. We will share our weeks in our partner house in Hilton Head with both families in the spring of 2006 and 2007. And in Menlo Park, Rob and Priscilla keep us updated on current politics and contemporary culture. Our little expanded family is filled with people we love and care

about. Jonathan and I both got so much more than we bargained for, and for which we are deeply grateful.

[83] Venerable Henepola Gunaratana, **Mindfulness in Plain English** (Boston: Wisdom Publications, 1992), 11. First published in Taiwan, 1991.

[84] Ayya Khema, **Be an Island; The Buddhist Practice of Inner Peace** (Boston, Massachusetts: Wisdom Publications, 1999). The Hershey Family Foundation sponsored the printing of this book.

[85] Venerable Henepola Gunaratana writes about meditation: "Meditation teaches you how to disentangle yourself from the thought process. It is the mental art of stepping out of your own way . . . Meditation is not other-worldly." When we can disengage the old and tired logic circuits that have formed, almost by habit, it lets our intuition, our deep mind, emerge. (27)   He talks about the difference between Hindu and Buddhist meditation, stating that Hinduism is "purely concentrative . . . Within the Buddhist tradition, concentration is also highly valued. But a new element is added . . . awareness." (34) And there are many schools of thought . . . Vipassana is the oldest of Buddhist meditation practices.

[86] At death, letting go is the one thing we can still do. One isn't striving to get anything, one is striving to get rid of everything. There is nothing to achieve. There's only letting go.

[87] Jonathan made the invitations on his computer, I compiled the gift baskets, which he delivered just before guests arrived.   Prior to the evening dinner, I taught the teen age girls hired to serve how to properly set a table. We rented furniture, plants, and dishes in Ukiah and hired cooks for the parties, housing guests in a charming B & B on the ocean, with spectacular coastal views, near Anchor Bay.

[88] Our children and grandchildren all came, as did my sister, Nancy, her son and my nephew, Patrick, and Jonathan's brother, Dave and his wife, Kathleen, with Kanti, Jonathan's nephew, along with our friends in Sea

Ranch and several old friends of Jonathan's. Jonathan's mother got out of her bed in Honolulu and onto an airplane, with two caregivers, and danced with her son.

[89] By organizing and cooking a dinner for the family, and even inviting Tom, my ex-husband; orchestrating a rehearsal dinner at the Stanford Park hotel, personally preparing a luncheon for the family tea ceremony before the wedding.

[90] Once again, Dae had to take care of us, including my petulant sulk when the photographer spent too much time with Tom and his wife.

[91] Dae has met Gurumayi several times and has attended many programs at the ashram, including meditation intensives. She knew the power of the Siddha path. But Rob had stayed far away. Years ago, I had obsessed about Rob meeting Gurumayi, particularly when she visited Milwaukee. He refused, no matter my wheedling and whining. It took years before I could let go of this desire. Rob has walked his own spiritual path. But it has taken even more years for me to let go of being an overprotective mother. Jonathan regularly kicks me under the dinner table as I continue to suggest items for him.

[92] In **The Way of Passion**, his book on the Sufi poet, Rumi.

[93] Ayya Khema, **I Give You My Life: the Autobiography of a Western Buddhist Nun** (Boston, Massachusetts: Shambala Publications, 1997), 139. Her epigraph is a poem by Hermann Hesse, *Stages:*

"As every flower fades and as all youth
Departs, so life at every stage,
So every virtue, so our grasp of truth,
Blooms in its day and may not last forever.
Since life may summon us at every age
Be ready, heart, for parting, new endeavor,
Be ready bravely and without remorse

To find new light that old ties cannot give.
In all beginnings dwells a magic force
Guarding us and helping us to live. . . "

There are three more stanzas of this delightful work. The last is particularly pertinent for this book:

"Even the hour of our death may send
Us speeding on to fresh and newer spaces,
And life may summon us to newer races.
So be it, heart: bid farewell without end."

[94] In this endeavor, we were supported by our small, sweet AA group in Gualala, where we regularly attend meetings. (Jonathan began to attend AA in 2002, quite to my surprise.) This group of eccentrics is beloved to us. There is first and foremost our good friend, Thayer, a former TV journalist and a documentary film maker – articulate, dramatic, brilliant, and always available for service; Jim, the local dentist and comic, formerly from Marin County, who tried all the wild and crazy drugs available to his profession; Tim, the 80 year old silver haired, elegant corporate CEO, who is involved in the politics of Sea Ranch, as is his second wife, Dibby, a retired city planner running for director and the pillar of the women's AA group; Patty, a former convict and tattooed tough drunk who is getting her appraiser's license and raising her teenage daughters in a loving manner very different from her abusive background and former homelessness Then there is Rug, who survived radical chemotherapy, beating all the odds; Jim gave him new front teeth; and Lyle, a sewer supervisor in the local town, afflicted with emphysema and no longer able to work; Wink, all 6 feet 10 inches whose liver is ailing, and articulate Marie, with virtually no education and a history of violent abuse as a child, is gaining personal strength and making a career for herself . . . along with the food addicts who are so few they attend AA. A humble group, always a source of wisdom and compassion. We did attend one meeting of the Food Addicts – with only two other people. The secretary introduced herself six times – I'm Nita, and I'm a food

162

addict – before she read introductory passages, standing each time she started a new item. It was very funny, and sweet.

[95] Sogyal Rinpoche, **The Tibetan Book of Living and Dying** (San Francisco: Harper, 1993).

[96] While stories end, life goes on. I had one fear left – a fear of heights, particularly in small planes. Thus it should not come as a surprise that Jonathan and I began flying lessons in 2007. For him, this was the completion of a process that began in the 1960s, which became pragmatic in 2007 with the unexpected purchase of a plane. For me, it began as a one-time confrontation with fear – to see whether I would be able to fly with Jonathan; then the lessons became a mental and physical challenge. Now I am resurrecting a childhood hero, Amelia Earhart.

But that's another story, with some big revisions of the overall plan! With new settings, in Mexico, and the Monterey Peninsula! And the title of that story is Being 70! But it might not get written.